MW00642049

The Subversive Puritan

Roger Williams, Freedom of Conscience and Church and State

Mostyn Roberts

EP BOOKS (Evangelical Press)
Registered Office: 140 Coniscliffe Road, Darlington, Co Durham, UK DL3 7RT

www.epbooks.org
admin@epbooks.org

EP Books are distributed in the USA by:
JPL Books, 3883 Linden Ave. S.E.,
Wyoming, MI 49548

www.jplbooks.com
orders@jplbooks.com

First published 2019

British Library Cataloguing in Publication Data available

ISBN 978-1-78397-247-0

Other books by Mostyn Roberts:
Francis Schaeffer

In this engaging volume Mostyn Roberts provides us with an introduction to the life and theology of Roger Williams, as well as an encouragement to learn lessons from him on how to live in our own times. Mostyn deftly sets Williams in his historical context on both sides of the Atlantic without bewildering the reader with too many of the vicissitudes of seventeenth-century political history. As Mostyn shows, Williams held some views still rightly regarded as eccentric, but his theory of mere civility as a viable basis for society is very close to the contemporary 'two kingdoms' theology that finds that basis in natural law. Even for those of us unpersuaded by the two kingdoms project, Mostyn's work can only serve to help us engage thoughtfully over the question of an adequate foundation for civil society. And the story of Williams and his trials is itself fascinating and well-told: what an extraordinary challenge these people faced as they sought to construct societies from scratch on the other side of the world!

Garry Williams, Director, The Pastors' Academy, London

This new biography of the key Puritan thinker Roger Williams is most welcome. Like many pioneers, Williams had some quirks and oddities in his thought, which Mostyn Roberts' biography does not hide, but his clarity of thought about the necessary matrix of true Christianity was nothing short of remarkable and this is why he must be remembered. Drawing upon the latest research on the Puritan author, Roberts outlines the contours of his life with special focus on his thought about religious liberty and why it is so important today. An excellent and truly thoughtful volume.

Michael A G Haykin, FRHistS, Chair and Professor of Church History, The Southern Baptist Theological Seminary, Louisville, Kentucky

If you visit the famous 'Reformation Wall' in Geneva, Switzerland, you will see a huge statue of Roger Williams. Sadly, he is little known today. As founder of the first ever colony to allow freedom of conscience and religion, and author of one of the first landmark works defending religious freedom, Williams deserves to be better remembered. We now take it for granted that freedom of thought, conscience and religion are fundamental to a free society, and we look back with horror at the religious persecution and coercion of a past age. So we should honour Roger Williams, who suffered much for insisting that force never produces genuine faith, and that compelled worship is abominable to God. Mostyn Roberts has filled a real gap by providing us with this clear and comprehensive account of Williams' life and thought. Helpfully, he does not gloss over Williams' undoubted oddities and eccentricities, but through it all the essential courage and conviction of a great man shines out.

Dr Sharon James, author, speaker, social policy analyst for The Christian Institute

Mostyn Roberts' publication on Roger Williams brings to light the life of one of the least recognized of that great body of Christians known as the Puritans. His biography makes for riveting reading as Roberts ably traces the personal circunstances, historical settings and biblical thoughts of a man who in so many ways was instrumental in shaping the New World. This is not just a well written biography of Williams, but the author shows us in a very compelling fashion how relevant Roger Williams' thought is in order to help us today articulate a Christian view of such vital issues as liberty of conscience, tolerance, the relationship between church and state and a pluralist society. A very timely book. Highly recommended!

José Moreno Berrocal, pastor, author and conference speaker.

In this fascinating study we see Roger Williams as a man of his time, and ahead of it; a man in his place, and outside of it. Avoiding shallow overview and lazy assessment, Roberts rather gives us thoughtful analysis and careful application. He enables us to understand Williams in his context, engage with his strengths and weaknesses, and appreciate some of the issues of conscience, tolerance and liberty which continue to press hard into our present experience. Roberts offers no easy answers, but raises many helpful questions and offers much useful insight.

Jeremy Walker, Pastor, Maidenbower Baptist Church, Crawley

Contents

For HILARY *My Love*

Acknowledgements

I WOULD LIKE TO THANK VERY WARMLY PROFESSOR MICHAEL HAYKIN OF the Southern Baptist Theological Seminary, Professor John Coffey of the University of Leicester and Dr Robert Oliver, formerly lecturer in church history at London Seminary for reading the manuscript, checking my history and making corrective comments—any remaining errors are mine; Dr Sharon James for her interest and encouragement; the Evangelical Library, London, for allowing me generous use of their set of Williams' works; the church of which I am privileged to be the pastor, Welwyn Evangelical Church in Hertfordshire, England, for allowing me a sabbatical in 2016 during which I did much of the spadework for this book; Graham Hind and Evangelical Press for taking on publication and last but absolutely not least my wife Hilary and sons Nathaniel and Thomas for patiently bearing with time spent on Roger Williams in recent years.

Chronology

1603	Usual accepted birth date of Roger Williams (may have been as late as 1606)
1621	Enters Charterhouse School
1623	Attends Pembroke College, University of Cambridge
1625	Accession of Charles I
1628	Petition of Right
1629	Williams chaplain to the Masham family at Otes Manor, High Laver, Essex
1631	Roger and Mary Williams arrive in New England; called as pastor by Salem
1631–33	Serves church in Plymouth
1633–35	Acting teacher of church in Salem
1635	Order of exile by the court in Massachusetts
1636	Williams flees to avoid banishment to England; Providence, RI, founded
1638	First Baptist church in America founded in Providence

1642   Civil War begins in England

1643   Williams sails to England to get charter for Rhode Island

1643–44   Williams publishes: *A Key into the Language of America, Mr. Cotton's Letter Examined and Answered, Queries of Highest Consideration, The Bloudy Tenent of Persecution*

1644   Charter granted by Parliamentary committee; Williams returns to Rhode Island

1645   Williams publishes *Christenings Make Not Christians*

1647   Rhode Island Constitution agreed

1649   Charles I beheaded; Oliver Cromwell, effectively, governs until 1658

1652–54   Williams back in London; Williams publishes: *Experiments of Spiritual Life and Health, The Fourth Paper Presented by Major Butler, The Hireling Ministry None of Christ's, The Bloudy Tenent Yet More Bloudy, The Examiner Defended*

1658   Oliver Cromwell dies

1660   Accession of Charles II and the Restoration of the Crown

1663   Royal Charter granted to Rhode Island by Charles II

1672   Williams debates with Quakers in Newport and Providence

1675–78   King Philip's War

1676   Williams publishes *George Fox Digg'd out of his Burrowes*, his record of the 1672 debates

1683   Williams dies, sometime before March

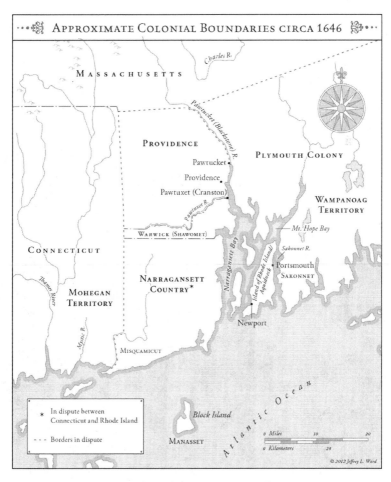

APPROXIMATE COLONIAL BOUNDARIES CIRCA 1646

Charles R.

MASSACHUSETTS

Pawtucket (Blackstone) R.

PROVIDENCE

Pawtucket

Providence

Pawtuxet (Cranston)

Pawtuxet R.

WARWICK (SHAWOMET)

CONNECTICUT

PLYMOUTH COLONY

WAMPANOAG
TERRITORY

Mt. Hope Bay

Narragansett Bay

Sakonnet R.

Island of Rhode Island Aquidneck

Portsmouth
SAKONNET

Thames River

MOHEGAN
TERRITORY

Mystic R.

NARRAGANSETT
COUNTRY*

Newport

MISQUAMICUT

Atlantic Ocean

* In dispute between
Connecticut and Rhode Island

- - - Borders in dispute

Block Island

MANASSET

0 Miles   10   20
0 Kilometers   20

© 2012 Jeffrey L. Ward

Map reproduced by permission of Gerald Duckworth & Co. Ltd

SOUTHERN NEW ENGLAND CIRCA 1675

VERMONT
(not under
English control)

NEW HAMPSHIRE

MAINE

Connecticut River

Merrimack River

Cape Ann

Salem

MASSACHUSETTS

Cambridge
Watertown   Charlestown
Boston
Charles R.
Merrymount

Massachusetts
Bay

Springfield

Plymouth

CONNECTICUT

Providence

Hartford

Warwick

Thames River

RHODE
ISLAND

Cape Cod

Aquidneck Island/
Portsmouth

Connecticut River

Mystic R.

Newport

New London

New Haven

Martha's
Vineyard

Nantucket
Island

Block Island

NEW YORK

Atlantic Ocean

0 Miles   20   40
0 Kilometers   40

© 2012 Jeffrey L. Ward

Map reproduced by permission of Gerald Duckworth & Co. Ltd

Introduction

'HE DID BREXIT BEFORE YOU GUYS,' SAID A STUDENT IN PROVIDENCE, Rhode Island, pointing to the outsize statue of Roger Williams overlooking the city. It was July 2016, a month after the United Kingdom's EU referendum. The student knew his history. Whatever Brexit may mean for the UK, Roger Williams was a breaker away, an exit man.

Yet it was not because he wanted to be. With many Puritans he had gone to New England in the 1630s to be free to worship according to conscience. The church system being established there did not give him the freedom he had hoped for. Regarded as a troublemaker, he was exiled from Massachusetts. He founded the State of Rhode Island and Providence Plantations.

Williams did more than found the smallest state in the Union. He is more important for why he did things than for what he accomplished. His life touched on some of the most important events, he rubbed shoulders with some of the most important men and his big ideas touched on some of the most important concepts in British and American history. His motivation, indeed his obsession, was liberty of conscience. It buzzed incessantly. It did not let him rest easy with any kind of compromise. It made him difficult to live with. He was prepared to suffer rather than yield a point.

For Williams, liberty was not the kind of freedom regarded as fundamental to the American way-of-life. Neither was it the freedom of civil rights that Williams cherished and struggled for. It was, instead, freedom to worship God according to conscience. Any other freedom was secondary. Moreover, what Williams needed for himself, he knew other human beings needed too. He fought for freedom not just for those who agreed with him, but for men and women of all beliefs or none. He was no relativist as to truth but knew that truth could not be imposed on people. Liberty of conscience for all was the guiding principle of his life. 'Freedom of different consciences to be protected from enforcement was the principal ground of our charter ... [and is] the greatest happiness men can possess in this world,' wrote a representative group of Rhode Islanders in 1657.[1] Their charter, first granted in 1644 and confirmed by Charles II in 1663, made Rhode Island the only society in the civilized world at that time that recognized what Williams called 'soul-liberty.'

It was also, as the historian John Barry says, the first in the world that 'broke church and state apart.'[2] Separation of church and state was the second, and subsidiary, bee in Williams' bonnet. It was, in his opinion, the only way to ensure soul-liberty. It sounded outrageous in his day, but it was to become enshrined in the First Amendment of the United States Constitution a century and a half later.

History has given Williams mixed reviews. To some he is a hero, perhaps over-romanticized; to others, he is a minor eccentric; but to too many, he is virtually unknown. In 1909 the Reformation Wall was built in Geneva. Ten heroes of the Protestant Reformation are honoured there by statues. The

American representative, towered over by John Knox to his right, is Roger Williams, standing alongside Oliver Cromwell, William the Silent and others. It is fitting recognition of his place at the root of the tradition of soul-liberty.

Do we need to remember him today? I believe so. We are living in turbulent times. Christians in the west are conscious of losing their heritage, perhaps fearful for the future. How do we live with our deep differences? How shall we live—together? Should we enforce religious beliefs and practices on others—or allow them to be enforced on us? What are the limits of toleration? Does civil society require safety from being offended or must it demonstrate the willingness to put up with it in the cause of freedom? How do we show confidence in the gospel and allow Word and Spirit to do their work freely? To what extent should the church look for support from the state? What is the nature and value of a Christian culture?

While the majority of the book is given over to the story of Williams' life, in the closing chapters I will seek to address three questions that particularly absorbed Roger Williams and which still concern us today: first, is liberty of conscience something we should treasure and protect? Second, what should the relation be between church and state? Third, how important is religion to the existence and stability of a society?

Williams is a difficult man to grasp. He is distanced from us by time. He is distanced by environment; he lived on the Wild West frontier long before Hollywood tamed it. He is distanced from us because he was of his age; once we feel we have grasped his age, Williams is then distanced from us because he was also not of his age, in some ways very far ahead of his age, and in some ways simply idiosyncratic. He was not an academic who only wrote about freedom, but was a man of study *and* action; even his greatest book was not written in the comfort of a study but in scraps of time torn from a hectic visit on political business to England in the midst of the Civil War.

He not only thought and wrote, however; he lived his principles. He sought (too hard we might say) for purity in the church yet was able to live with the roughest and most difficult of people in civil society. He held firmly to his love for God, to the Bible, to his pursuit of the knowledge of the God whom he had known since he was a child; and he founded a state where other men and women of all faiths and none could live without being 'troubled for conscience.' He disagreed with their beliefs; but they were entitled to share with him the common air of creation. He was right, very right, on some things; he was very wrong on some things too. But he still speaks to us today.

My aim in writing has been, first, simply to introduce Williams to many who do not know about him. It is surprising to realize that while he is one of the most studied figures in pre-revolutionary America, he is not commonly known today. It would be rewarding to rectify that a little.

Second, we can learn from him. The Christian foundations in the west are rapidly crumbling—many would say, have crumbled. Where they were accustomed to being hosts, Christians now feel themselves to be guests and unwelcome ones at that. They are having to rethink their relationship to the state, their attitude to other religions, to competing ideologies, to fierce and unscrupulous opposition. They are conscious of losing their Christian heritage and culture. Williams would have questioned the meaning of such ideas. Moreover, he lived for a time under a government aspiring to create the most Christian society ever known and he could not tolerate it, nor it him. He set about building a state with no established religion and with freedom of conscience for all. He believed that that was more truly Christian than the Christendom of the Middle Ages and of his day. In other words he was not only content to live in a culture where Christianity did not enjoy any kind of pre-eminence or privilege— he wanted to create a society that was explicitly pluralistic. Such thinking at least poses a challenge to our very natural tendency to lament the loss of a Christian past. As Williams once said of his own day, we are living in 'wonderful searching, disputing, and dissenting times.'[3] That kind of excitement about the opportunities of our day could become infectious.

Third, as a lifelong non-conformist I would like non-conformists to remember some of the root ideas of their own faith though they will see much in Williams they will not recognize and probably would not want to own. But we would be healthier if we remembered why our forebears believed what they did and acted as they did.

Finally, Williams believed in the liberty, under God, of the individual conscience, of the church and of the state. Any assumption of authority by one person or institution over another has to be rigorously justified, and strenuously challenged if illegitimate. Any lively Christian will want to promote ('propagate' was a popular word in Williams' day) the gospel; Williams firmly believed that universal liberty of conscience and the separation of church and state was the most healthy climate for gospel prosperity. I happen to agree.

Roger Williams does not give us all the answers to these questions. His life and beliefs, however, do lay a creative foundation for starting the discussion. As the western liberal consensus comes under strain there is also interest in him in recent scholarship. In the last twenty years Edwin Gaustad has published two short biographies and John Barry a major one. Timothy Hall has investigated his ideas on church-state relationships and James Calvin Davis his moral theology. James P. Byrd Jr. has contributed a study of how Williams used the

Bible. American academic lawyer Martha Nussbaum enlists a very secularized version of Williams in the cause of preserving America's tradition of religious equality. Os Guinness has revived his call for liberty of conscience. Theologian Miroslav Volf hails him as a model of religious exclusivism combined with political pluralism. Not to be outdone, Williams himself has contributed a new book—scholars in Rhode Island have translated a book he wrote in shorthand in his last years. Most recently, Oxford political theorist Teresa Bejan compares and contrasts Williams, Thomas Hobbes and John Locke in search of a basis for 'civility' in our disagreements, preferring Williams for his 'unapologetically cacophonous and evangelical approach to toleration.'[4] As the west re-examines its roots for a way in which we can live together with all our differences, it seems that Roger Williams is at least worth introducing to the table.

Chapter 1

Early Life

ROGER WILLIAMS WAS BORN IN LONDON AROUND 1603. HIS FATHER, James Williams, was a merchant tailor—more of a cloth merchant than a man who made clothes. His mother, Alice, hailed from St Albans, Hertfordshire. His older siblings were Sydrach and Catherine; the baby of the family was Robert. They lived in Long Lane, then Cow Lane, in Farringdon Ward 'without the city wall.'

Little is known about Williams' boyhood. It is a reasonable conjecture that he inherited some trading ability from his father, for it was by trading that he lived in New England. Perhaps proximity to London docks sparked a fondness for voyaging and the readiness of seagoing metaphors in his writings. There were refugee Dutch groups in his neighbourhood; it is possible that he picked up early knowledge of Dutch from them—later he would be able to pass on some of this to John Milton. Maybe from the way they were treated, he also saw something of the reality of religious persecution. Smithfield was a place renowned for the burning of heretics. In 1612 a young man called Bartholomew Legate was burned there for heresy—the last man in England, bar one, to die for heresy in this way.

The family attended the local parish church of St Sepulchre's where Captain John Smith was a parishioner. Maybe Williams was aware of the excitement when Pocahontas and her Native American retinue came to London in 1616. As the son of middle-class parents it is likely that Williams would have received some decent schooling but we have no details.

The world around Williams

The England into which Williams was born was a Protestant nation, though far from at peace with itself. In 1517 Martin Luther had ignited the revolution that we call the Reformation. Europe was divided between Protestants and Catholics. Protestants in turn were either Lutheran (northern Germany, Denmark, Norway and Sweden) or Reformed, who gave allegiance to theologians like John Calvin and Heinrich Bullinger (parts of Switzerland, Scotland, Hungary, the Netherlands and England). The Reformation in England had been spiritually quickened by John Wycliffe's English translation of the Bible in the fourteenth century and more imminently by William Tyndale's translation of the New Testament, but it was given institutional shape and vigour by the marital ambitions of Henry VIII. In divorcing Catherine of Aragon, Henry, between 1529 and 1534, pushed through legislation which effectively wrenched England from the Pope's domain.

Henry however was hardly Protestant—just his own sort of Catholic who made himself 'Supreme Head in earth of the Church of England.' His son Edward VI was very much a Protestant, and his short reign saw England surge towards a sort of Calvinism. His older half-sister Mary succeeded him and the nation lurched bloodily back towards Catholicism. But her reign too was short.

Elizabeth, daughter of Henry and Anne Boleyn, eventually settled the country in Protestantism as 'the only Supreme Governor [not Head] of this Realm ... as well in all Spiritual or Ecclesiastical things or causes as Temporal.' Subjects swore loyalty to her in that office by an Oath of Supremacy. An Act of Uniformity in the same year (1559) required all subjects to attend weekly worship at their parish church; 'recusancy,' failure to attend worship or even refusal to participate in the full liturgy, became a crime and a subversive act.

There was, then, some stability but not grassroots peace. Elizabeth died in March 1603. That summer James VI of Scotland was crowned James I of England. Roman Catholics did not disappear overnight. The most famous plot in British history, Guy Fawkes' attempt to blow up the Houses of Parliament, was foiled while Williams was a toddler. In the two decades prior to Elizabeth's death over one hundred Catholic priests were put to death, as were people accused of helping them.

But there were Protestants too who were unhappy. Elizabeth's settlement did not please those who wanted a more thoroughgoing Reformation. Many men had studied in Geneva and wanted to see more Calvinism and less Catholicism in the church, and worship conducted according to biblical precedent. Some were content to stay within the Church of England and work for reform patiently. Of these, some, led by the Cambridge scholar Thomas Cartwright, were proposing an alternative system, called Presbyterianism, after the Geneva model, which would have replaced sole bishops with government by elders and denied the monarch's right to govern the church. Men who were prepared to fight for reform from within became known as Puritans. Yet others were unhappy about waiting and wanted to worship outside the established church if it would not change. Robert Browne published *A Treatise of Reformation without Tarrying for Any* in 1582; in 1593 Henry Barrowe, John Penry and John Greenwood were hanged for denying the authority of the Queen in all matters relating to the church. Such ecclesiastical dissidents were called Separatists. It is known that there were a number of small groups of Separatists meeting in the Smithfield area of Williams' boyhood.

When James became king one of his first tasks was to try to satisfy the complaints of the Puritans. A group had met him on his way from Scotland with the Millenary Petition signed by approximately 1,000 ministers. It suggested that the sign of the cross should be removed from the baptismal ceremony and that the marriage ring was unnecessary; that the words 'priest' and 'absolution' should be 'corrected,' the rite of confirmation abolished, and the priests' cap and surplice—vestments of conformity—should not be 'urged.' At the Hampton Court Conference, convened to discuss these issues, it quickly became clear that under James there was very little prospect of reform, and certainly little chance of any version of Presbyterianism, of which he had had painful experience in Scotland. 'No bishop, no king,' was his motto.

Separatists fared worse than those who sought reform from within the church. In 1607 a group originally from Gainsborough, but who had moved to Scrooby in Nottinghamshire under William Brewster, John Robinson and William Bradford, left for Holland. Settling at Leiden, but eventually unhappy with Holland and despairing of returning to England, all but Robinson headed west for Virginia in 1620 on the *Mayflower*. They landed further north, near Cape Cod and settled the Plymouth Plantation. In later years these Plymouth pilgrims and Roger Williams would get to know each other well.

Also in 1607 another group of Separatists, from the same Gainsborough congregation, also meeting in Nottinghamshire, left for Amsterdam under John Smyth, a former fellow of Christ's College, Cambridge. A layman called Thomas Helwys accompanied him. Smyth had been influenced by Browne and Barrow but also came under the influence of Dutch Mennonites, spiritual descendants of the Anabaptists of the previous century. In 1609 he decided to baptize himself and then others of his congregation, thereby creating the first English Baptist church, though in Holland.

Smyth died in 1612 having declared in a statement of faith that 'The church of Christ is a company of the faithful; baptized after confession of sin and of faith.' No parish system for them; and no place for infant baptism. In the same statement he penned the first claim for full religious liberty in the English language:

> [We believe] that the magistrate is not by virtue of his office to meddle with religion, or matters of conscience, to force and compel men to this or that form of religion, or doctrine, but to leave Christian religion free to every man's conscience, and to handle only civil transgressions (Rom. XIII., 3, 4), injuries and wrongs of man against man, in murder, adultery, theft, etc. for Christ only is the King, and Lawgiver of the Church and conscience. (James IV. 12).[1]

Thomas Helwys shared Smyth's Separatist theology but not his association with the Mennonites. He led his congregation back to England and founded the first Baptist church on English soil in Spitalfields, outside the walls of the city of London, in 1612. This and Smyth's church in Amsterdam were General Baptists (Arminian in their theology); Particular Baptists (Calvinistic in their theology) originated in Separatist congregations in London and formed their first churches in the 1630s.[2]

In 1612 Helwys published *A Short Declaration of the Mystery of Iniquity*. In it he writes, 'The king is a mortal man, and not God, therefore hath no power over the immortal souls of his subjects, to make laws and ordinances for them, and to set spiritual Lords over them.' This was the first book in England making the demand for universal religious liberty—freedom of conscience for all.

Unsurprisingly, Helwys spent the last three years of his life in prison, dying in about 1615 in Newgate. His successor as the leader of the English Baptists was John Murton. He was cut from the same cloth. 'Earthly authority belongeth to earthly kings,' he wrote in 1615, 'but spiritual authority belongeth to that one spiritual King who is KING OF KINGS.' It is the foulest of crimes, he insisted, to force people's 'bodies to a worship whereunto they cannot bring their spirits.'

It was with a letter from Murton smuggled out of prison in 1620, pleading against persecution for cause of conscience, that Roger Williams began his great work *The Bloudy Tenent of Persecution*, published in London in 1644. We shall return to this later. There is no evidence that during his teenage years Williams had any contact with Separatists but emanating from these groups were the ideas that he would make his own and apply to explosive effect in the New World.

An influential mentor

We left Williams on the assumption that he had received a thorough education in his boyhood. Things really began to take off for him when he came to the attention of one of English history's great men and arguably England's greatest lawyer, Sir Edward Coke. Coke was a parishioner at St Sepulchre's and it may have been there that he saw the young Williams, perhaps thirteen or fourteen, taking notes in shorthand. A note written by Coke's daughter Anne Sadleir in 1652 informs us that:

> This Roger Williams when he was a youth would in a short hand take sermons, and speeches in the Starchamber and present them

to my dear father, he seeing him so hopeful a youth, took such liking to him that he put him into Suttons Hospitall and he was the second that was placed there.

Sutton's Hospital was Charterhouse School, founded by Thomas Sutton in 1611. Shorthand had been introduced into the country in 1588 and by the early 1600s schools were teaching it to pupils. Whatever the exact circumstances, Coke was struck by this boy and his shorthand and took him on to take notes of cases in the Star Chamber and Privy Council.

Sir Edward Coke was born to fight tyranny. He learned his law under Elizabeth; he was appointed Solicitor General in 1592 and as Attorney General from 1594 he prosecuted Sir Walter Raleigh in 1603 and then the Gunpowder plotters. In 1606 he became the guardian of the common law as Chief Justice of the Court of Common Pleas; in Bonham's Case he repeated the principle of Magna Carta that the king was under the law. In 1613 he was transferred to being Chief Justice of the King's Bench, dealing with the cases where the king was involved. James and Coke's arch-enemy Sir Francis Bacon hoped that this would bring him to heel but there was little chance of that. He was dismissed in 1616 and thereafter, while continuing legal work, he gave more time to politics as an MP. He led the parliamentary attack on crown monopolies. In opposing the infamous *ex officio* oath in the prerogative Court of Star Chamber and ecclesiastical Court of High Commission, by which inferences were drawn from silence, he insisted against Bacon and the king that 'no man may be punished for his thoughts,' for, 'it hath been said in the Proverb "Thought is free."'

In 1628, when Coke was 76 and Charles I was king, he was largely responsible for the Petition of Right which was a kind of statutory Magna Carta which enshrined (amongst other things) the right not to be taxed without Parliamentary approval, the principle of *habeas corpus* (no arbitrary arrest) and the right not to have soldiers billeted in one's house. An Englishman's house, as Coke said, is 'as his castle.' Together with Magna Carta and the Bill of Rights of 1689 the Petition of Right is regarded as one of the three main documentary pillars of the British Constitution.

He was just the tough-minded man England needed in an age where the king believed that he was accountable to God alone and even if he ruled badly his subjects should not resist him. To rebel against him was to rebel against God. Suffering and prayer were the subjects' proper response. James happily listened to advisers who told him that 'The monarch is the law; the king is the law speaking,' and, 'The King being the author of the Law is the interpreter of the Law.' 'No he isn't,' said Coke, with Magna Carta and 400 years of common law precedent behind him. James' son Charles would hold his father's views, with more piety but less political sense.

It was Coke that the teenage Roger Williams served as secretary and clerk from about 1616 to 1621. Although the majority of this time would not have been during Coke's years as Chief Justice, it is impossible to think that living so close to a man of Coke's ilk, central to legal and political affairs in those turbulent days, did not have a profound influence on Williams. John Barry perhaps makes too much of this, suggesting that Williams' convictions about the inviolable conscience came almost exclusively from Coke's influence. This is to neglect Williams' own reasoning on the subject and the prior weight of the Bible and theology in Williams' later thinking. Nonetheless, being assistant to a man who devoted his life to opposing the absolute ambitions of the king burned something deep into the young Londoner. You can also see something of where America came from. Indeed Coke's judgments were applied in American courts in the years leading to the War of Independence although exactly how influential they were is a matter of debate.

The relationship between Coke and Williams was evidently very close. In a letter to Coke's daughter Anne Sadleir in 1652, Williams wrote that her 'dear Father was often pleased to call me his Son, and truly it was as bitter as death to me,' when he (Williams) had to sail for America without the opportunity of saying goodbye to his mentor. He wrote later that in America 'how many thousand times since have I had the honourable and precious remembrance of his person, and the Life, Writings, Speeches and Examples of that Glorious Light.'

Sadly Anne Sadleir did not respond with her father's affection. Williams was an enemy of the church and the monarchy she loved. She returned, unread, books he had sent her asserting that what caused most bloodshed was leaving 'to every man's conscience to fancy what religion he lists.' But then, perhaps only Williams, having already received one rebuff, would have sent her *The Bloudy Tenent*. Before her death she wrote on the back of one of Williams' letters that 'if ever he has the face to return into his native country, Tyburn may give him welcome.'[3] Traitors were hanged there.

It is worth mentioning another possible influence on Roger Williams, namely Sir Francis Bacon. Francis Bacon and Coke spent most of their public lives at loggerheads, but Bacon was the brilliant mind behind a new approach to science, the root of the modern scientific method. In *Novum Organum, The New Organon or True Directions Concerning the Interpretation of Nature* (1620) he argued that progress in knowledge was better made through observation and experiment rather than by the Aristotelian and Scholastic reliance on logic from first principles. His insistence on experimentation opened a new world for science and was responsible for the establishment of the Royal Society.

Did this have any influence on Williams? John Barry argues that Williams' approach to truth owes much to Bacon. One example would be his use of the kindness and courtesy he found among the Native Americans to support his arguments for separating church from state. The state had no place imposing private beliefs and morality except when it affected civil peace—and look—actually it does not need to!

Williams does quote Bacon in his prefatory address to the Houses of Parliament in *The Bloudy Tenent*; he had obviously read something of him; he calls him 'the learned Sir Francis Bacon;' he was certainly very observant and analytical as shown in his first book *A Key into the Language of America*. But what influence Bacon's scientific method had on Williams is difficult to assess.

We are on firmer ground as we move on with Williams' life. In 1621, shortly before Sir Edward Coke was imprisoned by James I for nine months, he and Williams parted company, but on good terms. Coke had arranged for Williams to attend Charterhouse, a newly established school in Smithfield in the City of London.

Chapter 2

Student, Chaplain, Pilgrim

FROM THE AGE OF FIVE OR SIX WILLIAMS WOULD PROBABLY HAVE BEEN educated in some Smithfield classroom. He would have been 'initiated into his Rudiments'—reading and religion. Religion meant Bible history, the Catechism in English and Latin, prayers four times a day and on Monday morning questions to ascertain what he remembered from the Sunday sermon. Later he would learn grammar, English and Latin. In due course numbers and writing were added. Repetition was the method of learning with an examination on Fridays when the boys would ask each other questions on their week's lessons.

The next stage would probably have been a grammar school but there is no record of where this might have been. Latin would have been the medium of such education. Exercises in confuting and questioning each other sharpened the mind and the accusatorial and interrogative instincts. Puritan combativeness was provided with the weapons of its warfare in the elementary education of the time.

We know that Williams' early education must have been satisfactory because when he was entered for Charterhouse his fitness as a scholar was tested by examination. There he read only 'approved authors, Greek and Latin,' using his Greek New Testament (the only book provided by the school) in chapel. The tone of life was religious—Church of England religious, of course.

In July 1624 he was considered 'fit for learning' at Cambridge University and was voted an 'exhibition' to continue annually if he acquitted himself creditably. This sum of sixteen pounds was not a scholarship earned by academic distinction but an allowance to all those who by examination were adjudged capable of further study.

Cambridge

Roger Williams was admitted to Pembroke Hall (now College), Cambridge, simply under the name 'Williams' in June 1623 with nothing about his date of birth, parentage or previous school. His formal matriculation (entrance into the university) was in June 1624, a year later. One assumes that this first year provided in some way the basis for Charterhouse to grant him his exhibition in July 1624.

Pembroke was one of the oldest Cambridge colleges. Even by the sixteenth century, great names had already passed through its doors: the Marian martyrs John Rogers, John Bradford and Nicholas Ridley, who had been Master of the College; the poet Edmund Spenser; and the scholar and churchman Lancelot Andrewes who had also been Master. By 1623 however Pembroke was not a Puritan institution like, say, Emmanuel College under its Master, John Preston. Andrewes' influence had made Pembroke strongly Anglican and anti-Puritan. This would have pleased Sir Edward Coke, but it meant the young Williams was receiving his education in an environment hostile to Puritanism and what, at least towards the end of his time there, must have been his own developing convictions.

The Master when Williams was admitted was Matthew Wren. The chapel at Pembroke consecrated in 1665 was one of the first buildings designed by his nephew Christopher. According to Pembroke records Williams became a Watts Scholar in 1625; this benefaction had been established by Thomas Watts, a former archdeacon of Middlesex under Elizabeth. Scholars had to show wit and memory; likelihood of academic perseverance; a good disposition to 'true religion and the ministry ecclesiastical;' mastery of Greek and Latin languages and texts, with Hebrew grammar; fair handwriting; and a sound grasp of Calvin's catechisms. Perhaps this gives us the clearest insight so far into the kind of mind Williams had. Yet—a good disposition to 'true religion and the ministry ecclesiastical?' In a strongly Anglican college? It does not sound as if Williams at this stage had evinced the radical tendencies that would, within a decade, estrange him not only from the Anglican Church but from many of his fellow Puritans.

Williams left no record of his university years. His studies would have been based on the traditional 'trivium'—grammar, logic and rhetoric—with theology, especially Calvin's. He would, as Samuel Brockunier says, have 'had the art of disputation hammered into' him.[1] Studies would have been pursued with the agenda that orthodox Christianity was to be believed, supported and defended against Arminianism and Popery.

In the wider world, religious issues dominated politics. There was great joy in October 1623 when Prince Charles did not marry the Catholic, Spanish Infanta; gloom in 1625 when three months after his accession to the throne he married the French, equally Catholic, Henrietta Maria. James' 'Directions' in August 1623 forbade preachers from meddling in politics and warned bishops to be more circumspect in licensing preachers. In 1626 the unpopular Duke of Buckingham, the favourite of both James and Charles, was appointed Chancellor of Cambridge University in the face of fierce opposition.

Williams took his BA degree in July 1627. He felt able to sign the Subscription which required agreement to the king as Supreme Governor of the Church of England, to the Book of Common Prayer as containing nothing contrary to the Word of God and to the Thirty-Nine Articles of 1562.

Williams remained at Pembroke for another eighteen months, till the end of 1628. Sir Edward Coke was at the pinnacle of his political career, declaiming that 'Magna Charta is such a fellow that he will have no sovereign,' and introducing the Petition of Right.

Williams left before attaining his MA. By February 1629 he was chaplain in the Puritan home of Sir William Masham at Otes Manor, High Laver, Essex. His exhibition from Charterhouse was suspended later that year, the Governors noting that 'contrary to the orders of the Hospitall' Williams had ceased studying at Pembroke.

It is not known why Williams left Pembroke two years before his MA would have been awarded. Perhaps his convictions had changed and he would no longer be able to 'subscribe' as he had at the end of his BA. Such subscription would have been acceptable to a Puritan who was content to remain within the established church, but not to one with Separatist leanings. William Laud was in the ascendancy and perhaps Williams could not see himself serving in his church. Possibly the offer of a chaplaincy had come and was too tempting—which presupposes that his views were now at least Puritan. Being a man who, as he wrote later in life, enjoyed 'study and action,' the time had come for the latter.

Whatever the reason, he left Cambridge for Essex and, with it, the academic world for the homely, pastoral and political. At this point the momentum of his life began to pick up.

Spiritual life

I have said little about Williams' spiritual life. There has, in truth, been little to say. In his many writings, Williams rarely mentions his youth. In a rather sad but ambiguous phrase in a letter written when already in America in 1632 to John Winthrop, he wrote 'Myself, but a child in every thing (though in Christ called, and persecuted even in and out of my father's house these 20 years).' Glenn LaFantasie suggests that this is probably a scriptural allusion meant to 'emphasize the pervasiveness, and not the literal location, of the persecution RW had experienced as a suffering Christian. It is unlikely that RW meant he had been persecuted for his beliefs in the house of his father, James Williams.'[2] We cannot be sure exactly what Williams meant except this: at the age of about 29 he dated his Christian experience back twenty years, and he had been conscious of persistent persecution for his faith.

Altogether more hopeful is a sentence in his introduction to *George Fox Digg'd out of his Burrowes* in 1673: 'The truth is ... from my Childhood (now above three-score years) the Father of Lights and Mercies touched my Soul with a love to himself, to his only begotten, the true Lord Jesus, to his Holy Scriptures, etc.'[3] Puritans would have known exactly what he was talking about. He knows God as a gracious God; he knows him as Father; he knows him through Jesus Christ his only Son; he knows the grace of God experientially in his life; he knows that salvation is initiated by God; in his heart has been planted a love for the Scriptures. That is quite an anatomy of conversion in a short sentence! 'Above three-score years' would also fit in with a conversion age in his pre-teens.

Williams is tantalisingly silent about his theological and spiritual development as a young man. All we know is that in 1627 on receiving his BA he was willing to honour the king as Supreme Governor of the Church of England and agree to the Prayer Book and the Thirty-Nine Articles; by mid-1631, on his arrival in New England, he refused to accept the offer to be the teacher of the church in Boston because he 'durst not officiate to an unseparated people,' that is, a church not sufficiently separated from the Anglican Church.[4] During this time, then, Williams' theology shifted from Anglican conformity by way of Puritanism to an extreme form of Separatism.

Turbulent days

As a chaplain Williams would have been formally a Church of England clergyman but, employed in a private household, he would have been protected from the harsher aspects of the ecclesiastical climate.

These were turbulent days in church and state in England and Williams was to find himself in the midst of them in Essex. 'Commons' (the House of Commons) was coming of age and, like a feisty adolescent, was flexing its muscles against an increasingly intransigent and unreasonable royal parent. In 1621, led by Coke, they had presented a Protestation to King James asserting Parliament's right to debate 'the arduous and urgent affairs concerning the King, State and Defence of the Realm, and of the Church of England, and the maintenance and making of laws and redress of mischiefs and grievances which daily happen within this realm,' and to do so with 'freedom of speech.' In 1625 James was succeeded by his son Charles who caused dismay, as already mentioned, by marrying the Catholic Henrietta Maria of France. Charles shared his father's belief in the divine right of kings (that is, that the king is answerable to God alone) and, with even less sensitivity to his subjects' feelings, asserted his royal power at the expense of Parliament to steer the Church of England in an increasingly Roman Catholic direction.

On the political front the catalyst for confrontation was taxation. Parliament limited the customary grant of customs duties for the king's ordinary expenses (tonnage and poundage) to one year only. Charles resorted to a 'Forced Loan' and imprisoned prominent 'Refusers,' largely from the gentry class who were typically royalty's supporters. He imprisoned them without charge. Writs of *habeas corpus* were issued. The king's jailers refused to honour them. Soldiers and sailors were billeted in private homes because the army and navy had no money. Charles was provoking a constitutional crisis.

A fundamental principle was at stake: was the king above the law, or under it? Did he legislate at will, or as one element of a constitutional mobile whose balance had to be delicately maintained? Was he bound by the law or could he override whatever hindered him? These struggles would, in a few years' time, plunge England into civil war, but ultimately make Britain a parliamentary democracy with her freedoms far more secure though never to be taken for granted. Shipped across the Atlantic by the Puritans, shorn of the heritage of England's monarchical centuries, they would make America a nation that gloried in yet greater freedom.

In 1628 Charles, under pressure, assented to the Petition of Right that preserved political liberties. The king then promptly ignored it, ordering the Petition and his agreement to it to be 'made waste paper.' In March 1629, after further clashes, Parliament dramatically passed, with the speaker held physically to his chair, the Remonstrance, which branded anyone who encouraged Roman Catholicism or Arminianism or advised or paid the levy of tonnage and poundage without the consent of Parliament as an enemy of the state and kingdom. Charles dissolved Parliament and began eleven years of Personal Rule.

The religious turmoil was precipitated by Charles' catholicizing of the Church of England. The queen, Henrietta Maria, celebrated mass in her household. English Catholics joined her. The assassination of his favourite, the Duke of Buckingham, in 1628 drove Charles closer to her. He advanced ministers who preached the royal prerogative or denounced Calvin. Rails were introduced in some churches to separate clergy from lay people. Charles came to see Puritans as the enemy both in church and state. He insisted on strict implementation of practices that James had been wise enough to consider indifferent. Charles' Lord High Treasurer, Chancellor of the Exchequer and Secretary of State were secret Catholics. Arminian sympathizers (though they did not admit to it) gained high office. Puritans took the view that 'an Arminian is the spawn of a Papist.' The argument was not just about predestination or the extent of the atonement. Arminianism has a weaker view of man's depravity, a higher view of his capability to at least contribute to his salvation. Calvinists saw the connection between that and Catholicism. In the end man's power is exalted, God's sovereign grace reduced; glory goes to man, not to God. That was intolerable to the Puritans (nearly all of whom were Calvinists).

Charles' agent in religious affairs was William Laud who was appointed Bishop of London in 1628 and became Archbishop of Canterbury in 1633. Preaching was reported on and limited to forbid 'all further curious search' on doctrinal issues; the communion table was moved to the east end of the church and renamed the altar. The Puritans demanded simplicity according to Scripture, not the sign of the cross and wearing the surplice; Laud gloried in crosses, stained glass windows, formal ceremony and what he called 'the beauty of holiness.' Puritans wanted the Word to be free and worshippers to be free to hear God speak. Laud wanted worship to be according to the Prayer Book, conformity to man-made forms and ceremonies. John Milton complained that Charles 'bemoans the pulling down of crosses and other superstitious Monuments, as the effect of a popular and deceitful Reformation. How little this savours of a Protestant.'[5]

In 1629 Alexander Leighton attacked bishops as 'un-Christian and satanic.' Held in an open prison (that is, open to the elements, not with unlocked doors), for fifteen weeks, he was then lashed with thirty-six stripes and had 'SS' ('Sower of Sedition') branded on his face. His nose and ears were sawn off. Then he was sent to prison for life. Life could be quite short in prison.

Laud considered that religious conformity was essential for the welfare and indeed survival of the state, 'It is impossible in any Christian commonwealth that the church should melt and the State stand firm.' Most Puritans would have agreed with him. 'As religion is decayed, so the honour and strength of this nation decayed,' said Francis Rous. Probably unintended by Rous, there is even here an important distinction: religion is not quite 'the church' and 'the nation' is not quite 'the state.' But in principle the main issue was not the separation of church and state, but what kind of church and what theology England should have. The Puritans wanted a purified Protestantism; Charles and Laud wanted a re-Catholicized Protestantism.

The Commons noted in February 1629 a dangerous design 'aiming at the subversion of all protestant churches of Christendom.' They decided they had to take on Charles and Laud. Robert Barrington wrote, 'We have brought the business of religion ... and against both popery and arminianism ... into the house and with one consent ordered that it should be the main business and first agitation.' One may not want to deal with religious matters in Parliament—but if the king is Supreme

Governor of the church and, moreover, pushing his agenda—what can one do?

The letter containing this statement was given to Roger Williams to take back to the Masham home in Otes. Williams was a close observer of affairs and trusted messenger of one of the foremost Puritan families in Essex (and therefore in the country) in the turbulent years of 1629 and 1630.

There were other causes of turmoil in England. The economy was crumbling. The textile industry was buckling under pressure from superior Dutch technology. In May 1629 weavers rioted in Essex. Almshouses filled with old labourers. New owners of previously open lands or royal forests threw people off the land. People flooded into cities, especially London whose population doubled from 200,000 to 400,000 between 1603 and 1649. Beggars abounded. Plague was a regular occurrence. More people died in London than were born in it—growth came from population influx—a situation that continued to the late nineteenth century.

Protestants were also depressed by news from the continent. Their armies were retreating before the Catholics across Europe in what would be known as the Thirty Years' War. The view of a Parliamentary committee in 1629 was that Protestants in Germany and France were 'in great part already ruined,' and Ireland 'almost wholly overspread with Popery.' The great (though brief) days of Gustavus Adolphus were as yet in the future. Morals too were lax. James had legislated in his *Book of Sports* for maypoles and dancing on the Sabbath. Charles would re-issue this in 1633. Meanwhile the Puritans saw around them drunkenness, bear- and bull-baiting and sexual immorality. It was a gloomy, even a desperate, time to be a conscientious Protestant. But the men leading the opposition to the king were not revolutionaries by nature. They believed in the monarchy. They wanted to be loyal to their monarch. Mostly they loved the Church of England too—but not the Arminian, Catholic version that Charles and Laud wanted.

One further turn of the religious screw by Laud was to require family chaplains to be approved by a bishop. The High Commission already made it impossible for new Puritan clergy to find a church post. Puritans had found openings in the homes of sympathetic gentry. Just before this loophole closed, Roger Williams became family chaplain to Sir William Masham.

Chaplain in Essex

The Essex to which Williams came from nearby Cambridge was a hotbed of Puritanism. Sir William Masham was a lawyer and member with Coke of Inner Temple. With his father-in-law, Sir Francis Barrington, and brothers-in-law, Robert and Thomas Barrington, he served with and supported Coke in Parliament. With Sir Francis he had gone to prison rather than pay the Forced Loan. Sir Francis' wife, Lady Joan, had gone to prison with her husband. Sir Francis died shortly after his release. The widowed Lady Joan of Hatfield Broad Oak was a formidable matriarch accustomed to welcoming to her home visitors active in politics including her nephews the young Oliver Cromwell and Edward Whalley, future regicides (signers of the king's death warrant). Living not far from the Masham residence at Otes were Puritan ministers and leaders and promoters of the New England enterprise, such as Thomas Hooker, John Winthrop, Hugh Peter and John Eliot. With Sir William Masham, Lady Joan supported seventeen clergymen under pressure from Laud; minsters dedicated books to her; the Earl of Warwick told her that in judging a clergyman he would 'sooner your recommendation than all the bishops in this kingdom.' Close to these influences, in the Masham-Barrington network, was an exciting place for a young, bright graduate of decidedly Puritan leanings.

The Masham household was not small. It had fifty-three rooms, every room furnished, servants to match. There was a brewhouse, a malthouse, a dairy, a cheese loft; there were barns, granaries, orchards, fields and animals. It was akin to a small village rather than a modern private home—even a stately one. Records of the time indicate the kind of work a chaplain might be expected to do. The lady of the house concerned for her soul might seek his help as she engaged in private prayers, mournings to God for pardon, Bible readings, self-examinings, twice daily public prayer in a family chapel and his personal attention to talk and pray with her as she sewed, assisting her as she wrote out her spiritual exercises, reading from the Bible or Foxe's *Acts and Monuments* (*Book of Martyrs*).[6] It appears that the lady of the house, Lady Elizabeth Masham (daughter of Lady Joan Barrington) was not too demanding, but Williams' life would have been busy nonetheless as he sought skilfully to shepherd anxious souls on their way to heaven.

It is to this period that we owe the first two surviving letters we have from Roger Williams. During this time he formed the intent of marrying a young lady called Jane Whalley, cousin to Oliver Cromwell. Regrettably Jane was of a social standing considerably above Williams; doubly regrettably, she was the niece of Lady Joan Barrington. Lady Joan's permission had to be sought. Williams wrote, pleading his cause and confessing himself 'altogether unworthy and unmeet for such a proposition.' Lady Joan agreed: he was unworthy. Stung to the quick, Williams showed a trait that would manifest itself often enough in later years. He did not know when to stop. He wrote again to Lady Joan, accompanying the expression of his obvious, bitter disappointment with pastoral advice. There are times to give pastoral advice to elderly ladies, occasions when warnings about their spiritual state would be fully appropriate, but probably not when you are deeply upset by their refusal of a niece's hand in marriage. She was close to her everlasting home, he wrote; her, 'candle is twinkling and glass near run out. The Lord only knows how few minutes are left behind.' She should waste no time in repenting, for 'the Lord hath a quarrel against you.'[7] Such admonitions were not uncommon from conscientious chaplains, and even the mark of a faithful watchman—but not the best approach to Lady Joan from Williams at this juncture!

Thankfully Williams had 'friends at court;' Sir William Masham considered him 'a good man and good friend.' He and Lady Elizabeth pleaded for Lady Joan to be reconciled to him. It was hard work. Williams at this point became very ill, close to death, and only then was there some softening of the breach that gladdened the Masham hearts.

The Lord healed too. Williams' second letter to Lady Joan is dated May 1629; by late autumn he was married to Mary Barnard (or Bernard), a lady's maid at Otes Manor and the daughter of a Puritan clergyman, Richard Barnard. Mary was to be Williams' loving and faithful companion throughout his life. Only a year or so of that life was to be spent in England. Jane Whalley meanwhile married another Puritan clergyman, William Hooke, who evidently did win Lady Joan's approval. She spent twenty years in Massachusetts with him before returning to England with their eight children in 1654. Hooke returned in 1656 and became a chaplain in Oliver Cromwell's household.

There is an intriguing statement in Williams' first letter to Lady Joan, referring to an offer of a ministry in New England.[8] He was not taking it up. But it reminds us that to be Puritan in those days was to be close to talk of emigration and colonization. The Barrington family was particularly interested in settlements in the West Indies. Roger Williams however was less interested in prospects for trade as in freedom to minister and worship according to conscience. He had had one known meeting with

Thomas Hooker and John Cotton, at, or in connection with, an important meeting of the Massachusetts Bay Company at Sempringham, Lincolnshire in July 1629. He doubtless had many similar discussions. This meeting was significant because in later recollection of it he remembered challenging the senior clergymen on their use of the Book of Common Prayer; he 'durst not join with them in their use of Common prayer' he later wrote.[9] This was a different Williams from the one who had signified agreement to the Prayer Book in 1627.

His conscience was his guiding light. In his letter to Sir Edward Coke's daughter many years later he wrote that 'when Bishop Laud pursued me out of the land and my conscience was persuaded against the national church and ceremonies' he had to flee without saying farewell to Sir Edward, as 'I durst not acquaint him with my conscience and my flight.'[10]

The Massachusetts Bay enterprise declared in its original charter that 'the propagation of the gospel is the thing we do profess above all to be our aim in settling this Plantation.' This would have appealed to Roger Williams who expressed his desire in later writings as 'That which I long after, the natives' souls.'

In March 1630 John Winthrop, lately appointed the new governor of the Massachusetts plantation, set sail on the *Arbella* with other ships and 1,000 settlers for New England. In December that year Roger and Mary Williams joined them on the *Lyon*, arriving in February 1631.

Chapter 3

New England

FOR NEARLY A CENTURY AND A HALF AMERICA HAD ATTRACTED TRADERS and settlers from Europe. The Spanish, French, Portuguese, Italians and Dutch had explored, developed trade and established plantations (later called colonies). England was a little behind. Only after Spain, bloated with South American gold, became the most powerful nation in Europe, did England see the pressing need to compete in the Americas. Not only trade and wealth, but also the defence and propagation of the Protestant religion, were the great incentives. In the 1580s Sir Walter Raleigh tried but failed to plant settlements in Roanoke, North Carolina. Raleigh paid Richard Hakluyt to write of the possibilities of the New World and his *Principall Navigations, Voiages and Discoveries of the English Nation* published in 1587 inspired many. In 1607 Jamestown, Virginia, became the first lasting English plantation. But it was hard going. Thousands went to the New World, and thousands died. But they persevered and slowly established footholds.

Meanwhile news came of fertile lands to the north of

Virginia but south of the fruitful fishing and fur trading fields of Newfoundland. The government encouraged colonization, allowing joint stock companies to find investors, raise money and sponsor adventures to land English claimed in North America. In 1620 James granted the newly created Council for New England all the land between the fortieth and forty-eighth parallels—roughly between Delaware Bay and the St Lawrence River, to subdivide and charter colonies within this region.

The first permanent settlers however were unauthorized. Puritans saw in the New World the possibility not only of trade but of freedom—freedom to worship according to conscience, and in a way not imposed by the Church of England. Separatists had left England for Holland in 1608. In 1620 some of these, under William Brewster and William Bradford, left for Virginia but landed near Cape Cod. These hundred or so Pilgrim Fathers of the *Mayflower*, counting among their number Church of England adherents and irreligious adventurers as well as devout Separatists, established the Plymouth Plantation.

Plans were afoot though for a settlement about forty miles further north. In 1626 settlers founded Naumkeag. In 1628 the Massachusetts Bay Company was formed, its patent procured by Sir Robert Rich, a Puritan leader and friend of the Masham-Barrington network, now head of the Council for New England in place of Sir Fernando Gorges and a key figure in matters of American colonization. Most of the members of the Massachusetts Bay Company had Puritan sympathies. They wanted not only trade; they wanted to create a Puritan haven in New England. They sent fifty planters or settlers to Naumkeag with the combative John Endecott as governor. The settlement was renamed Salem, which meant 'Peace.' Although Williams does not specify, it is likely that it was from the Bay Company, who were looking for teachers and ministers for Salem, that he received the invitation while he was still in England in 1629; an invitation which he refused. This was not to be the last invitation he rejected.

At the time Parliament was dissolved in March 1629, the Bay Company received a royal charter, confirming the earlier charter from Sir Robert Rich and the Council of New England, to the region between Plymouth colony and present-day New Hampshire. The Company sent 350 more settlers in five ships to Salem. They arrived in June. Most of them settled slightly further south in what they would call Charlestown. Meanwhile in England two important meetings of the Bay Company took place. In London it was decided that the government of the plantation should be transferred to those who resided in New England; also that the charter itself, the physical document, should be transferred to the settlement. This was a step of enormous significance; it changed an investment company into a true colony which could pursue its own interests. A document to hand could not be forfeited to a possibly hostile government; it could more easily be amended if circumstances demanded; and with the government situated in the colony itself, decision-making would be better informed, quicker and more accountable.

The second important meeting was the one previously referred to, in Sempringham. John Winthrop, Thomas Hooker, John Cotton and Samuel Skelton, already to be one of the ministers at Salem, with others, proceeded with plans for the actual settling, financing and governing of the colony, and the conversion of the Native Americans. Roger Williams may have been at this meeting; he certainly knew men who were there and was doubtless familiar with their deliberations. They agreed that creating a commonwealth of the godly was the primary goal of the settlement. They would carry only godly people 'of good rank, zeal, means, and quality,' no troublers of Israel, or hangers on and no adventurers pursuing foolish ambitions.

What would the relation of the new settlement be to the Church of England? The Bay Company determined that unlike Plymouth Separatists they would remain loyal to the mother church. At least, that is what ministers Francis Higginson and Samuel Skelton said before leaving England. However, geography can affect doctrine. In Salem they agreed that the authority to call a minister resided in a local congregation—a group of believers 'joined together in covenant.' Full church members were only those who signed this covenant. Skelton was appointed pastor, Higginson teacher. Elders laid on hands. Bay Company ministers did not wear the surplice, kneel, make the sign of the cross, use the Book of Common Prayer. It may not have been Separatism; but neither was it Church of England—certainly not Laud's version of it. In fact two brothers called Browne were expelled from the colony and sent home by governor Endecott for using the Book of Common Prayer in private assembly. The Bay Company in England admonished Endecott.

The Puritan vision

John Winthrop was a godly man, an industrious lawyer, affectionate husband to each in turn of his three wives (the first two died), and a caring father. He was not exciting or charismatic; he exhibited the qualities of an elder (1 Timothy 3) to a high degree. Distressed at events in church and politics and struggling, as a farmer at Groton, Suffolk, with the economy, he reluctantly determined to emigrate. His son John Jr. and his wife followed. Like other Puritans he grieved that his homeland 'grows weary of her inhabitants.' Puritans wanted to be loyal to the Church of England; they did not want to become Separatists. They did not want to go to Holland which even Separatists had abandoned as not offering a fit home for their posterity. To battle on in England was becoming a commitment to permanent and apparently fruitless struggle, not to speak of the dangers to life, limb, family and property. Their great instrument, the House of Commons, had been dissolved. But America offered opportunity: 'The whole earth is the Lord's garden,' he wrote, 'and He hath given it to mankind with a general commission (Genesis 1:28) to increase and multiply and replenish the earth and subdue it.' The gospel of Christ could be carried to other lands to raise up a bulwark against the kingdom of Antichrist being erected by the Jesuits. Protestantism was being brought to desolation in all Europe. Many saw the troubles in Europe as but the beginning of the judgement of God on his unfaithful people, England surely to follow. The founts of learning, Oxford and Cambridge, were corrupt and licentious. A minority but growing number of Puritans saw themselves as at the beginning of the Last Days and as participants in the opening skirmishes of the last battle. Carrying the gospel to the Native Americans not only offered them salvation but brought the end of the world closer by taking the gospel to the ends of the earth. Two decades later similar eschatological thinking would motivate Puritan leaders to allow the Jews to settle in England.

In August 1629 Winthrop and a dozen leaders of the Bay Company signed a solemn pledge to emigrate. A date was set, 1 March 1630. Winthrop would be the new governor, replacing John Endecott. From then on Winthrop threw himself into the exhaustive and detailed planning involved in taking 1,000 people in eleven ships to New England. Yes, they wanted people of Puritan persuasion but they needed skilled carpenters, brickmakers and shipwrights and many other skilled workers. Not everyone could be expected to be Puritan. Provided they were sympathetic they would be welcome; many poor servants and tradesmen were paid for by the wealthy.

On 20 March 1630, the *Arbella*, bearing Winthrop, with three sister ships, ahead of the rest, weighed anchor off Southampton. Delayed at Yarmouth until 8 April they finally left England for the New World. But not before hearing two sermons.

A city upon a hill

The emigrants had gathered, probably in Southampton. A thousand of them, predominantly of Puritan conviction, many anxious, some desperately sad to be leaving, others more excited by prospects of a new beginning. Some were conscious of guilt— was now the time to be leaving England? Were they really just running away? But again—they were taking the gospel to a New World, the true gospel, not a Papist message, and 'savages' could hear and be saved.

John Cotton preached 'God's Promise to his Plantation.' He drew largely on 2 Samuel 7:10 (KJV), 'Moreover I will appoint a place for my people Israel, and will plant them, that they may dwell in a place of their own, and move no more.' Cotton was a great and popular preacher from Boston, Lincolnshire. He was not leaving now but had come to say farewell to emigrants from his parish. Cotton had survived Laud's attentions so far by a certain flexibility. He used selected parts of the Book of Common Prayer and an assistant conducted the sections of the service Cotton objected to. When challenged over refusing to kneel he wrote an apologetic letter saying he had reconsidered his position. But he was being watched and the net was tightening. In September 1633, fleeing for his life with Thomas Hooker and Samuel Stone, he too disembarked in New England, at the port named after his home town, Boston.

In March 1630 he told his Southampton congregation that emigration was justified. The old land could not support them. To occupy vacant land was justified, 'to plant a colony ... and settle a

City or Common-wealth elsewhere.' They were to feed the Native Americans with their 'spirituals.' They would be a new Chosen People; God's people. But with privilege comes obligation. 'If you rebel against God, the same God that planted you will also root you out again,' he preached.

John Winthrop preached the second sermon. Some think this was preached on board the *Arbella* but others that it was more likely preached at embarkation or shortly before. Wherever it was preached, it was one of the most significant sermons, at least in terms of its historical consequences, ever preached. While Cotton was more intent on giving the emigrants reassurance, Winthrop wanted them to know very clearly what was expected of them in the New World. Historian Francis Bremer suggests that it sets out many of the key elements of the Puritan view of society: awareness of community and individual interdependence, awareness of the various callings of men and a sense of mission.[1]

Remember that it was no part of the general Puritan vision to separate from the Church of England. Winthrop and those with him, unlike the *Mayflower* emigrants who had settled further south in Plymouth a decade earlier, strongly desired to remain attached to their nation and church, though a purified church. Indeed on leaving England, Winthrop and the other Bay Company settlers had been at pains to assure those they were leaving that they were not Separatists. 'We desire ... to call the Church of England ... our dear Mother,' they declared. The reasons for leaving England were not merely political or economic, nor even to escape religious persecution and seek freedom. There was a strong positive sense of mission. This was what Winthrop wanted to express in his sermon.

He entitled it *A Modell of Christian Charity*. It sets out the strong sense of New England being a new Israel, with the conviction that

God has both commissioned them and established a covenant with them.

He spoke first about Christian love and argued that all that God has given is for the common good, hence a nation is a commonwealth; that different vocations are like different parts of the body, fitting each other so that society works harmoniously; every man has need of the other. Moreover, this is not just to be an outward conformity and sociability, but love is the bond that makes the work perfect. If the settlers were to have the comfort of being in Christ then they must exercise this kind of love.

The second theme of the sermon was the covenant between the emigrants and God. They had become God's chosen people, like Israel. But with privilege comes responsibility. For three reasons in particular, preached Winthrop, the Lord, though he is patient for the time being with those who are not his people, will not bear with us in our failings: first, because of the marriage covenant; we are nearer him and so he is more jealous of our love and obedience. As God told Israel, 'You only have I known of all the families of the earth: therefore I will punish you for all your iniquities' (Amos 3:2, KJV); second, he will be sanctified in those that come near him as with Nadab and Abihu (Leviticus 10); and third, when God gives a special commission he looks to have it strictly observed in every article as Saul was to observe God's instructions against Amalek but did not (1 Samuel 15). He concluded:

> Thus stands the cause between God and us. We are entered into covenant with Him for this work. We have taken out a commission. The Lord hath given us leave to draw our own articles ... We have hereupon besought Him of favour and blessing. Now if the Lord shall please to hear us, and bring us in peace to the place we desire, then hath He ratified this covenant and sealed our commission, and will expect a strict performance of the articles contained in it; but if

we shall neglect the observation of these articles which are the ends we have propounded, and, dissembling with our God, shall fall to embrace this present world and prosecute our carnal intentions, seeking great things for ourselves and our posterity, the Lord will surely break out in wrath against us, and be revenged of such a people, and make us know the price of the breach of such a covenant.

Now the only way to avoid this shipwreck, and to provide for our posterity, is to follow the counsel of Micah, to do justly, to love mercy, to walk humbly with our God. For this end, we must be knit together, in this work, as one man. We must entertain each other in brotherly affection ... We must uphold a familiar commerce together in all meekness, gentleness, patience and liberality. We must delight in each other; make others' conditions our own; rejoice together, mourn together, labour and suffer together, always having before our eyes our commission and community in the work, as members of the same body. So shall we keep the unity of the spirit in the bond of peace. The Lord will be our God, and delight to dwell among us, as His own people, and will command a blessing upon us in all our ways, so that we shall see much more of His wisdom, power, goodness and truth, than formerly we have been acquainted with. We shall find that the God of Israel is among us, when ten of us shall be able to resist a thousand of our enemies; when He shall make us a praise and glory that men shall say of succeeding plantations, 'may the Lord make it like that of New England.' For we must consider that we shall be as a city upon a hill. The eyes of all people are upon us. So that if we shall deal falsely with our God in this work we have undertaken, and so cause Him to withdraw His present help from us, we shall be made a story and a by-word through the world ... And to shut this discourse with that exhortation of Moses, that faithful servant of the Lord, in his last farewell to Israel, Deuteronomy 30. 'Beloved, there is now set before us life and death, good and evil,' in that we are commanded this day to love the Lord our God, and to love one another, to walk in his ways and to keep his

Commandments and his ordinance and his laws, and the articles of our Covenant with Him, that we may live and be multiplied, and that the Lord our God may bless us in the land whither we go to possess it.

This was not new theology for Puritans or indeed for Englishmen. John Foxe in his *Book of Martyrs* three quarters of a century earlier had made the stately homes and humbler firesides of England familiar with the idea that England was a chosen nation, indeed had replaced Israel as God's covenant people. In *Areopagitica*, his masterpiece arguing for freedom of the press in 1644, John Milton would write 'God is decreeing to begin some new and great period in his church ... what does he then but reveal himself to his servants, and as his manner is, first to his Englishmen?'[2] The deliverances from the Armada in 1588 and the Gunpowder Plot in 1605 were seen as special covenantal favours by God: 'It is the Lord who delivers England,' said Thomas Hooker. But in return—being a covenantal God, the Lord required much of England. She had to fulfil her covenant obligations. John Winthrop saw it as his obligation to use his gifts to build abroad what could not foreseeably be established in England—a new commonwealth of Israel. He was a new Moses; Deuteronomy was an obvious text to apply as he spoke to people on the verge of entering the Promised Land.

This of course is a wonderful vision and Winthrop's sermon was printed and widely distributed. It was however a sermon to a congregation of the largely faithful. What happened when that congregation became a nation? It is a fine vision for a church, but is it going to work as a blueprint for a commonwealth, a political entity, a state? What happens when members of the congregation are unfaithful? What happens when even the faithful profoundly disagree? Will the vision for an assembly of people gathered by faith and covenant suffice for harmonious dwelling together in a new country? Will it authorize the exercise of authority over malcontents and miscreants? What happens when people with a different vision come flooding in?

Roger Williams was to profoundly challenge the Puritan status quo on these issues. He argued trenchantly that no nation could be in the same place in relation to God as Israel had been; that no nation could be in covenant with God; that moreover church and state should be separated to a far greater extent than he saw in New England; and that all people should have freedom to worship according to conscience. These issues comprised the great ideological and theological cleavage that divided Williams from Winthrop and the settlers in Massachusetts.

Chapter 4

Godly Minister or Troubler of Israel?

ON 12 JUNE 1630 THE *ARBELLA* ANCHORED OFF SALEM. IT IS ESTIMATED there were about 500 inhabitants in New England at that time. Three hundred and fifty emigrants came on these first four ships. Before 1640 between 15,000 and 20,000 would follow. The 1630 influx found settlers struggling for survival. 'About ten houses lined a dirt street, heading up a hill from the water; the handful of other buildings were little more than huts and hovels,' writes John Barry.[1] Many lived in wigwams like the Native Americans. John Winthrop found little time to write to Margaret. His son Henry who had accompanied him drowned within a few days of arrival. Winthrop went exploring. He decided to make his headquarters at Charlestown, twenty miles south of Salem, only to move before September to a better fresh water supply at nearby Boston. William Blackstone already lived here. He eventually left Massachusetts to the Puritans saying he had left England to escape the rule of the Lord Bishops and now had no desire to live under the Lord Brethren. Samuel Maverick had a fortified home on Noddle's Island in Boston Harbour; and nearby was the licentious Thomas Morton whose lifestyle was markedly un-puritan and he let the Puritans know it.

Boston was soon to become the economic and political centre of the colony.

Winter was coming; settlers were already dying. Winthrop had to make plans. He showed the qualities of leadership the members of the Bay Company had seen in him and which were to make him loved and respected in the years ahead even when not all his actions met with approval. He sent Master William Pierce of the *Lyon* back to Bristol to get much needed supplies. He sent men up and down the coast and inland along the rivers to trade with Native Americans, to buy corn and to find provisions. That year, a harsh winter came, more bitter than any known before. God, it seems, was testing them.

Roger Williams arrives at Boston

On 5 February 1631 the *Lyon* anchored in Boston harbour. No doubt the greatest welcome was for the provisions; but John Winthrop noted also that 'Mr Williams, a godly minister,' was on board. Roger Williams and his wife Mary were in New England. Now Winthrop's model of Christian charity was to be tested.

The Bay Company had it seems tried to entice Williams to New England as a minister two years previously. Now another opportunity presented itself. John Wilson the minister of the Boston church was returning to England and would be away for many months. Williams was invited to take the position of teacher in the church. For Williams, no more than 28 (possibly younger) this was a wonderful opportunity. Yet he declined. 'I durst not officiate to an unseparated people,' he explained in a letter to John Cotton Jr in 1671.[2] He could not bring himself to join in or lead worship in a congregation who, while pure themselves, had not renounced fellowship with the impurity of the Church of England.

People liked Roger Williams. He was, as Edmund Morgan summarizes, 'a charming, sweet-tempered, winning man, courageous, selfless, God-intoxicated—and stubborn—the very soul of separatism.'[3] Winthrop, shocked to the core at his refusal of the offer from Boston, tried to win him round with reasonable argument but to no avail. Williams went on to express an opinion far more explosive than his rejection of the offer of a ministry. The civil magistrates, he said, had no authority to enforce 'the First Table,' the first four of the Ten Commandments: that you must not have any god before the Lord; nor make any graven image; nor take his name in vain; and must keep the Sabbath day holy. Effectively Williams was arguing that the state had no authority in religious matters. This was not just an attack on the regime in Massachusetts; it was an assault on the way government's responsibility in relation to religion was seen in England and throughout Europe, by Protestant and Catholic, by Puritans and even by many Separatists. Henry Barrowe, for example, the Elizabethan Separatist, had insisted that the state should destroy idolatry. But by 1612 Thomas Helwys, founder of the first Baptist church in England, wrote in *A Short Declaration of the Mystery of Iniquity*, that while the king has been given by God, 'all worldly power which extends to all the goods and bodies of his servants,' there is a kingdom that is not of this world and, 'with this kingdom our lord the king has nothing to do,' and has not, 'power to command men's consciences in the greatest things between God and man.'

It seems likely that Williams had had access to Helwys or similar literature. In the letter of John Murton, Helwys' successor, with which Williams begins his major work *The Bloudy Tenent*, Murton argues, like Helwys, that the laws of the civil magistrate extend no further than over a man's body or goods, and to that which is external; over the soul of man God will not suffer any man to rule.

Whatever the origin of Williams' thinking, his whole life's course was directed by this conviction. No-one struggled more persistently to navigate and chart the elusive and dangerous coastline of soul-liberty in relation to the authority of the state. No-one more consistently heeded the authority, under Scripture as he interpreted it, of conscience—even if, to others, his reasoning seemed obscure.

Salem

If, then, Williams closed the Boston door in his own face, what of Salem, up the coast? Higginson and Skelton had established a church there that was more separatist than the Boston church. When the Winthrop group had arrived from England they had refused them participation in the Lord's Supper because they did not belong to a covenanted church. They sounded like Williams' sort of people. They took a liking to Williams and offered him the position recently made vacant by Francis Higginson's death.

Boston objected, though without exactly telling Salem to withdraw the offer. Boston had no authority to object. But Salem did withdraw it. Roger and Mary Williams travelled south, arriving in Plymouth, still a separate plantation, in the summer of 1631.

Plymouth

Again, Williams was liked. Two governors of the colony spoke highly of him. William Bradford later described him as, 'A man godly and zealous, having many precious parts,' although he did add 'but very unsettled in judgement.' Edward Winslow called him, 'a man lovely in his carriage,' and, 'the sweetest soul I ever knew.' Williams became active in the church, 'prophesying' (preaching and exhorting rather than teaching) on Sundays. He became an unpaid assistant pastor. He worked the land and their first daughter, Mary, was born in August 1633. He maintained good relations with John Winthrop, evidenced in a letter from autumn 1632. He expressed delight that Massachusetts had decided not to allow ministers or elders to hold civil office. He wrote that he was not an elder 'nor ever shall be if the Lord please to grant my desires, that I may intend what I long after, the natives' Souls.'[4]

It was at Plymouth that Williams first made substantial contact with Native Americans. Mission to the Native Americans had always been a professed object of the English colonization projects; it was for example the first object of the Virginia Company. Puritans going to Massachusetts wanted to reach them—for their own sakes, to hasten the return of Christ and also to prevent them becoming Catholic under the mass conversion techniques of French and Spanish priests. The problem was that little was being done about it. Williams managed to establish a rapport with the Native Americans unmatched at that time by any of his countrymen.

Although most of his life would be spent among the Narragansetts of Rhode Island, he began in Plymouth getting to know the people, customs and language of the Wampanoags in that region. Williams was never romantic about Native Americans; he later referred to his dislike of their 'filthy smokey holes' and in anger referred to them as 'wolves with men's minds.' But he achieved a level of mutual trust and respect with them and a knowledge of their language that was not only unique amongst the English but was, in just a few years, and on other occasions, to be the means of averting bloodshed between the races. Williams' first book, completed on board ship for England in 1643, was nothing explicitly to do with the state, the church or politics but an anthropological and linguistic manual entitled *A Key into the Language of America.*[5] He had a deep empathy with the native humanity around him. Sometimes, as in *A Key*, he contrasted them, to the disadvantage of the English:

> If Natures Sons both wild and tame,
> Humane and Courteous be:
> How ill becomes it Sons of God
> To want Humanity?[6]

This was after his banishment from Massachusetts, as yet in the future. But in 1633 tensions were building up again. It was agreed in autumn that he should leave Plymouth after he fell 'into some strange opinions' according to Governor Bradford. Brewster expressed fears that Williams might 'run the same rigid course of separation and anabaptistry which Mr John Smith, the se-baptist, at Amsterdam, had done' ('anabaptistry' being almost the worst thing of which you could accuse a Protestant at that time). It worried Williams that settlers who returned to England had worshipped there with the national church and were not reproved for it when they returned. Perhaps more troubling were his developing views on the royal patent, the grant by which the Bay Company held its land. It was false, asserted Williams, for James, who granted the charter, to claim to be the first Christian king to discover these lands. Moreover, a king's Christianity does not give him a more valid claim to land than anyone else. Further, the land belonged to the Native Americans. Sensitized to the situation of the Native Americans from his two years in Plymouth, he called English colonization 'a sin of unjust usurpation upon others' possessions.'[7] Winthrop and John Cotton argued that there was enough land for everyone; and (their favourite argument), hadn't God removed thousands of Native Americans by plague before the emigrants arrived, leaving the land clear for them? Anyway, the Native Americans hunted and moved around and could not be truly said to 'own' any land. 'Nonsense,' said Williams and others who knew about their habits. The 'sachems' (chiefs) knew where the boundaries of their territories were. Their land should be paid for.

In truth, the settlers did usually purchase new land they obtained from the Native Americans, but Williams' views, particularly about the legitimacy of the King's Patent by which they held their first grant of land, and in effect calling the king a liar, worried the settlers. The last thing New England wanted was trouble with the crown.

Salem again

In 1633 on returning to Salem, Williams took up, by popular approval, but unofficially, the post of teacher that had been withdrawn from him two years previously. He had prepared a treatise, now lost, explaining his views on the King's Patent and Winthrop and others read it. They were concerned. A group of ministers and leaders in Boston and Salem talked to Williams and uncharacteristically, this time, he backed down but without changing his views. They accepted his submission. Crisis averted—for now.

Soon, with his fellow pastor Samuel Skelton, he was objecting to a fortnightly ministers' meeting, fearing it might grow into a presbytery or superintendency, to the prejudice of churches' freedom. In view of Salem's experience of Boston's interference over Williams in the past, they had reason to be cautious about ministerial influence. By 1637 there was a synod and superintendency that exercised just the kind of power Williams had feared.

There was debate too about whether women should wear veils (1 Corinthians 11:13); this was one Williams inherited rather than initiated but he was not reticent in agitating for veils. Other matters blew up, seeming trivial to us, but important to the settlers at that time. Sometimes Williams was not the instigator but received unfair share of the blame; sometimes he was, and had a good case supported by others. One example was the 'loyalty oath' which arose in the following way.

It was in late 1633 that William Laud became Archbishop of Canterbury, making him officially supreme (under the king) in the Church of England. Puritans were watched; sermons were reported on; Star Chamber, without the protection of the due process of common law suffered the fate of many 'prerogative' institutions and became synonymous with arbitrary oppression and cruel injustice. In February 1634 William Prynne lost his freedom and his ears. What had been a steady flow of emigrants became a flood, escaping Laud's introduction of 'downright popery' into the church. In 1635 of all emigrants to the Americas twenty-five per cent went to New England but of those who were from strongly Puritan areas such as Essex, ninety-five per cent went there. Puritans also went to Bermuda and Barbados. Up to 20,000 people emigrated during the 1630s.

Massachusetts began to flourish. It was, however, attracting unwelcome attention in England. Their clergy did not use the Book of Common Prayer, wear the surplice, nor allow crosses in any building. Yet they still professed to be reforming the Church, not separating from it. Some of those banished or punished by Massachusetts sought revenge in England. The original founder of the Council for New England, before handing over to the Earl of Warwick who gave the Massachusetts Bay Company its charter, was Sir Ferdinando Gorges. He now decided he wanted a piece of the action and a slice of the profits in New England. He sought in court the return of the Bay Company's charter. Rumour spread in New England of a military expedition from England against them. The colonists planned in April 1634 to build a floating gun battery in Boston harbour. A loyalty oath was required of all freemen (who at that time had to be church members) and also all non-freemen had to swear loyalty to the authorities in the colony. Later, in correspondence, John Cotton said this was 'offered' not imposed—well, an offer you could not refuse. If you refused twice you would be banished. The oaths, notably, did not mention loyalty to the king.

Williams objected to the oath so far as it applied to non-church members. 'A magistrate ought not to tender an oath to an unregenerate man,' for that would be to cause him 'to take the name of God in vain,' he declared. An oath was part of worship. Swearing an oath was a serious spiritual act. Moreover, to swear loyalty to an earthly institution such as the *state*, was to trivialize both true worship and God. His reasoning was not so much to keep unbelievers from having religion imposed on them; it was to keep the worship of God pure.

Meanwhile in summer 1634 the 'floating fortress' idea was dropped in favour of fortifying Castle Island in the harbour. It became known that Thomas Morton, the early settler whose estate the Puritans had by now destroyed, was taking action in court in England and that Gorges was indeed coming over with a fleet to recall the charter. The threat was real.

By August, after the death of Samuel Skelton, Williams was acting pastor of the Salem church as well as its unofficial teacher. When the General Court (the governing body) called a fast day, Williams declared that he had discovered eleven public sins for which God was chastening the colony. Less welcome was Williams repeating his conviction that the state should not enforce conformity to the first four commandments; he returned to challenging the legitimacy of the royal patent; the charter itself should be renewed—they should return to England to get a new one, he said.

Meanwhile the trained bands, local militia, were training in readiness. Salem's band was led by John Endecott, the former governor. All trained bands flew the red cross of St George. With his sword Endecott slashed the cross out of the flag. Puritans believed that any cross violated the second commandment. Even Winthrop had renamed a place called 'Hue's Cross,' 'Hue's Folly.' The fact that the cross of St George had been bestowed by the Pope did not help. A court met at the home of the then governor, Thomas Dudley. They considered Williams' recent opinions but at this point took no action. They decided on Endecott's action. A committee was set up and designed flags for the bands without the cross on them. Eventually, in March 1635, Endecott was punished by being debarred from office for one year. The colony was agreeing that the principle behind what he had done was correct—no crosses; but he had done it without due authority.

The court—remember, a state organ—also asked ministers to provide a set form of church discipline for use in the colony.

Ministers continued, at the General Court's request, to meet with Williams. The state stopped administering the loyalty oath. This was a big step in an age when the religious force of an oath was considered one of the bonds of society. Williams continued pressing—forced tithes were wrong, and payment of taxes to ministers, as 'No-one should be bound to maintain a worship against his own consent.'[8] The Salem church decided to call him formally as teacher. The magistrates and ministers, together, advised them not to. Salem called him. Salem's defiance was worse than Williams'.

Williams' causes (the oath, the patent, the cross) either initiated by him or adopted, may seem small to us, but as W. Clark Gilpin perceives:

Williams' thought began with the principle that the rites and symbols of proper Christian worship could be used only within a covenanted congregation. To require others to use them in any form not only forced those persons into sin but profaned the symbol.[9]

In June 1635 Gorges' ship broke apart on launching in England. Seeing this as God's favourable providence, the Puritans were reassured in their course.

Salem, wanting to expand, asked for land at Marblehead Neck. The General Court delayed consideration of this 'because they [Salem church] had chosen Mr Williams as their Teacher.' Political leverage was applied to deal with a judicial and church issue. Williams appealed over the head of government. He wrote to the other churches in the colony protesting at this interference with the church's independence in calling its own minister and using political power to block a legitimate claim. The churches refused to read out his letter. Williams protested at their not reading it. He urged the Salem church to separate itself, with him, from all the churches in the Bay.

That was a step too far for the loyal Salemites. They could no longer support him.

Positions hardened in August and September. As he had done at an earlier crisis in his life, when refused the hand of Jane Whalley, Williams fell seriously ill. He lost the use of his voice. He did not lose the ability to write. In due course he was summoned to appear before the General Court in October, all the Bay ministers required to be present. In later correspondence John Cotton stated what the charges had been against Williams and Williams never refuted his summary: they were Williams' complaints first, that the settlers did not hold their land by the King's Patent but that the natives were the true owners; second, that a 'wicked person' should not be called upon to take an oath; third, that the Puritans should not participate in Church of England services in

England; and fourth, that the civil magistrate's power extends only over the bodies and goods, not the souls of men.[10]

Williams was asked to recant; offered time to change his ways. He could not; he would not. On 9 October 1635 the court ordered that:

> Whereas Mr Roger Williams, one of the elders of the church at Salem, has broached and divulged diverse new and dangerous opinions, against the authority of magistrates ... and yet maintains the same without retraction, it is therefore ordered that the said Mr Williams shall depart out of this jurisdiction within six weeks.

The precise reasons for the banishment have been much debated. Were they religious or civil? Was he punished for disturbing the civil peace, or for his doctrines? John Cotton later argued that it was much to do with the matter of the King's Patent, that is, it was principally a civil matter; Williams was disturbing the state.[11] But that had been settled and not raised again for a year or so before the court's decision. Cotton also accused Williams of a 'violent and tumultuous carriage' against the patent and a 'heady and turbulent spirit' and his 'self-conceited, and unquiet, and unlamblike frame of spirit.'[12] The last straw was surely writing, over the ministers' heads, to other churches; and then separating from them, and trying to persuade his church to separate from them, 'which letters,' wrote Cotton in 1647, 'coming to the several churches, provoked the magistrates to take the more speedy course with so heady and violent a spirit.'[13] The real reason was no doubt a combination of these things. For some, no doubt, it was enough that he was a troublemaker and a threat to the nascent colony.

Because of the approaching winter and Williams' continuing illness the magistrates agreed to delay his banishment. Williams, however, had been ordered not to propagate his views, but within six weeks he was found to be teaching them in his home. The court decided not only to banish him from Massachusetts but to return him to England. John Winthrop (not, at this point, governor) heard of this and informed Williams. Three days before a ship's captain with fourteen men came to his home to take him to a ship for England, Williams slipped away into the Massachusetts winter.

Chapter 5

The New England Way

WHAT WAS THE METHOD OF GOVERNMENT IN THE BAY COLONY UNDER which Williams chafed? His crimes were the public proclamation of beliefs that were considered new and dangerous to the colony. Despite John Cotton's assessment of the banishment, it seems that the attack on the patent, which was the most obviously political attack from Williams, was not in the forefront of the court's mind in October 1635. When church and state are closely entwined, though nominally separate (and in New England probably more separate than anywhere in Christendom) to attack or question one is to undermine the other; heresy and sedition become indistinguishable. What Williams challenged was not the ideal of a godly society but the presupposition of the whole New England experiment set out in Winthrop's vision of a city on a hill, in which church and state worked towards the same goal. This may have been a godly community but, crucially for Williams, it was one where individual conscience was stifled. Any dissident was a threat. The motives of the oligarchy in Boston were good, no doubt, yet they were enshrining their orthodoxy as constitutionally unassailable; dissent was both sin and a crime.

Moreover, it was, after all, a very young colony. It was insecure for a number of reasons; the Puritans were trying to establish themselves in a new and dangerous environment; their leaders were educated, intelligent men, but they were trying to create a nation with Winthrop's controlling vision, the general terms of their charter and precious little else apart from the Bible and their experience of government in England. They had fled from a regime that had persecuted them and still sought to control them; they did not see themselves as rebels against the king or the church they wanted to reform. They wanted to be, and be seen to be, loyal subjects, so they were shaken by Williams' radical attacks on the legality of their title to the land and nervous about his perceived attacks on the king's integrity. They believed that state and church were separate but that nonetheless the state was the 'nursing father' to the church. Winthrop believed that; but then so did Laud. Williams did not. His conception of separation of church and state was much more radical. The limits of the state in spiritual matters in his view were far more tightly drawn than they were by the Puritans or almost anyone else at that point.

Winthrop and the charter

As Francis Bremer reminds us, the worldview on which the Puritans based their political structures was predominantly medieval.[1] John Winthrop's sermon contains most of the key elements of their view of society—their awareness of community and individual interdependence, their awareness of the various callings of men and their sense of mission. The sinner redeemed by grace, therefore, owed it to God and his neighbour to use his gifts for God's glory and his neighbour's good. The concept of calling was central. Calling gave you dignity and usefulness but also your place in life; covenant bound you to God and your neighbours.

Winthrop counted about fifteen members of the Massachusetts Bay Company in New England at the end of 1630. The charter granted authority to make all necessary laws so long as they were 'not contrary or repugnant to the laws and statutes of this our realm of England,' and, 'for settling of the forms and ceremonies of government and magistracy fit and necessary for the said plantation.' The members of the Company were known as 'freemen.' They were to meet in a 'Great and General Court' four times a year to make laws. Once a year they would elect a governor, a deputy governor and eighteen assistants to manage affairs between meetings of the General Court. This executive council was to meet every month. The governor or deputy and at least six assistants must be present at every Court; effectively seven men therefore could exercise all the powers of the Court. The two types of meeting, General Court and monthly executive, would be indistinguishable in membership.

Neither Winthrop nor his Puritan peers such as John Endecott and Thomas Dudley (father of the poet Anne Bradstreet) were democrats. They believed that God entrusted certain men in church and state with the authority and the gifts for government. Merely being born an Englishman did not give the right to take part in the political process. Yet the General Court meeting in Charlestown in October 1630 took the step of extending the term 'freeman' to all the settlers in Charlestown. Now 'freeman' described not only members of a commercial company but the citizens of a state, with the right to vote and hold office. However, their right to vote was limited to electing assistants (also called magistrates), and the assistants chose the governor and deputy. The assistants were, in this model, the 'legislators'; freemen as such had no authority in the law-making process. At the next

General Court, 116 persons were admitted as freemen, probably most if not all of the adult males, excluding servants, then in the colony. Moreover, a further stipulation was added that 'no man shall be admitted to the freedom of this body politic, but such as are members of some of the churches within the limits of the same.' To be a freeman, therefore, you had to be a church member. In a few years three quarters of the inhabitants of Massachusetts were excluded from civil privileges because they had not been accepted as church members.

Edmund Morgan is probably right in arguing that the reason Winthrop did this was to be found in the concept of covenant.[2] Puritans like Winthrop believed that it was of 'the nature and essence of every society to be knit together by some Covenant, either expressed or implied.' By coming to New England, the settlers had expressed confidence in their covenant with God to establish the colony. The involvement of the wider body of settlers was not a step to democracy, which Puritans as a whole despised, but a way of gaining explicit agreement and validation of a second covenant, establishing the government. Yet after determining the form of government and selecting the persons to rule them, the freemen's role was ended.

Further changes followed. There was discontent in Watertown when the government levied a tax for fortifications; 'no taxation without representation,' argued the town, in effect. The court thereafter agreed that two men from every plantation should confer with the governor and assistants about raising taxes. In 1632 the power to appoint the governor and deputy was transferred to freemen from the assistants. In 1634 the major weakness in Winthrop's scheme came to light when representatives of the freemen asked to see the charter and realized that all the freemen were to take part in legislating; freemen originally of course had meant only the members of the

Bay Company; Winthrop had extended the meaning of freemen to include all (male, adult, non-servant, church member) settlers, but not granted with that extension the power to legislate. It was agreed that rather than have an unworkable Athens-style democracy of all citizens meeting to vote on issues, they would appoint two deputies from every town as their representatives at the General Court.

In summer 1634 Thomas Hooker and others from Salem sought permission to settle in Connecticut. They were at first forbidden, though later permitted, but in the course of debate a 'negative voice' or veto over legislation became established for the assistants. This had little basis in the charter, but it was accepted and in effect created a legislature with two chambers, the assistants always being the 'upper house.' A clear line had to be maintained between governors and governed. The line, for Winthrop, ran between the assistants and the deputies, appointed as representatives of the people to the Court.

Winthrop's model of government was for as little as possible. He had set out his vision in *A Modell of Christian Charity*. Love was to be the bond of community. Biblical justice was to be the standard for society. One minister hoped that the Bay would 'endeavour after a Theocracy as near as might be to that which was the glory of Israel.' Whether the Bay was a theocracy depends on definition. If theocracy is defined as being a society in which the state and church were formally one, then it was not—but then, neither, on those terms, was ancient Israel because king and priest were distinguished and were not allowed to trespass on each other's domain. If theocracy is defined as being a society in which state and church were closely intertwined, however, and in which they shared the same vision of society and influenced and supported each other in pursuing a common goal by enforcing the same laws—then yes, New England was a theocracy. Moreover, the government was in the hands of the saints—only church members could participate in political life. Williams often said that despite formal separation of church and state, the Bay's church, congregational as it was, was implicitly a national church. New England wanted to honour God; it was a theocentric state. There were services during the week and two on Sunday; the government had to ban them on certain days for the sake of work. The Bible informed every activity. Ministers and church officers were not permitted simultaneously to hold civil office but they were constantly referred to for advice. It was said of John Cotton that 'Whatever he delivered in the pulpit was soon put into an Order of Court, if of a civil, or set up as a practice in the church, if of an ecclesiastical concernment.'

The laws applied by church and state were God's laws or based on God's law. Governments set wages and prices to protect the poor and the economy. They forbade the sale of firearms to Native Americans; they seized Richard Clough's strong water because he sold too much of it to other men's servants; they fined Sir Richard Saltonstall, a Bay Company member, for missing the first Court meeting. In 1636 Boston prohibited a resident from filing a lawsuit until the church had first heard the dispute.

The Puritan William Gouge said that 'a family is a little Church, and a little commonwealth.' The same basic principles apply in each society. Winthrop as a governor ruled the state as an elder might rule a church or a father a family—with firmness and love, seeking God's glory, applying God's law, training all those under his authority for godliness. Whilst the law of God was clear, discretion in applying it was of the essence of Winthrop's concept of government. In his hands it was patriarchal and paternalistic; in the wrong hands (and there were some among the early leaders) it could be a blueprint for autocracy. The freemen showed their confidence in Winthrop by voting him into office as governor in 1637, 1638 and 1639 (after a three-year break following the dispute about deputies in 1634) and again, after the *Body of Liberties* was accepted in 1641, from 1642 until more or less the end of his life in 1649. But the clergy wanted more definite limitations on the exercise of power. Through the deputies, over whom as members in their churches they exercised great influence, the ministers were able to exert influence on government. The deputies had as early as 1635 formed a committee to publish a code of laws 'in resemblance to a Magna Charta.' Winthrop, doubtless influenced by his understanding of the English common law, preferred a body of laws built up piecemeal, case by case. He recognized that the Bible could not be applied wholesale. Setting out a code would impose undue rigidity in the future.

John Cotton produced 'Moses His Judicialls' as a law code, providing that those who rejected correction by the church should be banished and that outright heretics should be put to death. The code was not adopted but these two provisions later appeared in Massachusetts statutes. Eventually Nathaniel Ward, now a minister but previously an experienced lawyer from London, produced in 1638 the *Body of Liberties*. It was formally adopted in 1641. A hundred provisions drew on Magna Carta, the Petition of Right and other laws of England, but always under Scripture, and tailored to meet the needs of the new commonwealth. There were fewer capital offences (twelve) than in England, based largely on the Ten Commandments—for example, worshipping a false god, blasphemy, adultery. Also punishable by death, on biblical principles, were witchcraft, murder, sodomy, bestiality, man-stealing, false witness and treason.[3] Monopolies were prohibited, freehold land tenure was encouraged as being according to the law of God; judicial procedure was simpler than in England.

Churches and church membership
Churches were gathered groups of saints. To knowledge of and

belief in the doctrines of the faith and an upright life the Puritans in New England added an insistence that the candidate offer proof of his election. It became a necessity for church membership that candidates could 'declare what work of grace the Lord had wrought in them.' By the end of the 1630s this requirement was well established in New England. Francis Bremer regards this restriction, or purification, of church membership as 'the most notable contribution' of New England to the Puritan movement.[4] In their organizßation too the churches were finding a new way. A group of Christians would select men regarded as 'pillars'—usually seven—who would agree a church covenant and then appoint a pastor and sometimes a teacher. Other officers included (sometimes) ruling elders and deacons. The New England Way in relation to the church was set out in 1648 in the *Cambridge Platform*. To provide a supply of educated clergy Harvard College was founded by the magistrates of the Bay in 1636.

Inevitably the churches took their responsibility of fostering godliness seriously. A member would be censured for sharp business practices; one was excommunicated for marrying a woman his church considered 'vain, light and proud ... and much given to scoffing;' another for idleness and being 'somewhat proud.' Church-going was compulsory though mostly it seems to have been willing. Services could be three hours long. Every adult was compelled to support church and ministry by payment of tithes, enforced by the state. After a church pronouncement of excommunication, the culprit had three months before the civil power dealt with him. Banishment from the state could follow, for offences such as heresy, including opposing infant baptism, or blasphemy.

The churches were 'congregational' in policy, free to choose their own officers, members and practices—though this was not always respected in practice as when Boston put pressure on

Salem in relation to Roger Williams. The New England Puritans, apart from one or two dissidents, wanted nothing to do with Presbyterianism on the one hand, or Separatism on the other.

Church and state

The goal of government in church and state was, it was assumed, to produce godliness. The two institutions used different means to persuade and had resort to different sanctions to punish, but that the two should work hand in hand was not questioned by the Puritans. Yet it was also insisted that church and state were distinct and should be kept separate. Men could not hold office in church and state simultaneously. The church is a spiritual institution and deals with things spiritually. The ultimate sanction is excommunication. The state however can use the 'sword,' including the death penalty or banishment. Like the church the state has a responsibility to uphold the true religion. If a heretic is a threat to stability—a fundamental concept for measuring social welfare—then the state should step in. Roger Williams and Anne Hutchinson were not punished for holding wrong views, but for publishing them. They were threatening the stability of society. Liberty was valued but as freedom to live God's way, and that meant in practice as defined by the government of the day. Freedom for antinomians, Anabaptists and other Enthusiasts, said Nathaniel Ward, was 'free Liberty to keep away from us, and such as will come, to be gone as fast as they can, the sooner the better.'

Despite their bitter experiences in England, the Puritans still wanted to leave the establishment and protection of the true faith in the state's hands. It would hardly have been possible for them to conceive of anything different. To have policy dictated to the state by the clergy would have been to give the church too much power over the state—the shade of Roman Catholicism.

Yet the two spheres closely co-operated. Magistrates frequently consulted the clergy; clergy had immense influence over the people through their preaching and they were still the best educated class in the community. The appointment of deputies gave them influence closer to the seat of government. In any event laymen such as Winthrop were at least as committed as any clergy to the religious goal of building a new Jerusalem.

The *Body of Liberties* established that the state could establish Christ's religion in every church. It could deal with the church members in civil things and the church could deal with civil officers for improper magisterial actions, but interestingly 'no church censure shall degrade or depose any man from any Civil dignity, office, or Authority'—that is, excommunication, for example, would not affect his standing as a magistrate. Loss of church membership by excommunication did not entail loss of freemanship.

The General Court blurred the church-state distinction by ordering, to produce 'good behaviour,' that anyone who was excommunicate but had made no effort to be restored, should be fined, imprisoned or banished for his obstinacy. In due time this was repealed. The church-state distinction was again crossed when one Hugh Bewitt was adjudged by the General Court, not a church, to be guilty of heresy. There were no church courts, but some ministers did want all criminal matters involving church members to be dealt with by them before coming to the state. The first priority with dissenters in either church or state was to bring them back into the flock. Admonition was employed to bring them to conviction (that is, to be convinced so as to repent of their sins). Ministers and magistrates had spent much time trying to persuade Roger Williams of his errors before eventually expelling him. If an individual continued in error, then he would be excommunicated from the church, perhaps also expelled from the colony. In 1630–31, the colony banished fourteen people, two per cent of its population. As Williams later wrote, the logical conclusion of a national church is that excommunication means banishment.[5]

The goal of godliness meant that government felt it necessary and justified to legislate, for example, for men to wear their hair short. To avoid heathen names, days of the week were known as the first or seventh (namely Sunday, or Saturday); and the months the first (March—until 1752) to the twelfth (February). People should get up early. A bell in Hartford, in next-door Connecticut, rang to wake people up an hour before daybreak.

Undesirables were warned off, kept out or excluded. Many of them would end up in Rhode Island, the colonial sink estate founded by Roger Williams.

Chapter 6

Rhode Island

IT WAS A HARSH WINTER INTO WHICH ROGER WILLIAMS SLIPPED ALONE IN January 1636. He left behind Mary and their two children (the second daughter, Freeborn, had been born in October). He wrote in 1670 that:

> When I was unkindly and unchristianly (as I believe) driven from my house and land, and wife and children (in the midst of New Engl. winter now about 35 years past) at Salem: That ever honoured Govr Mr Winthrop privately wrote to me to steer my Course to the Nahigonset Bay and Indians, for many high and heavenly and public Ends, encouraging me from the Freeness of the place from any English Claims or Patents.[1]

Williams took Winthrop's advice as a 'Hint and voice from God, and ... I steered my Course from Salem (though in Winter snow which I feel yet) unto these parts, wherein I may say as Jacob, Peniel, that is I have seen the Face of God.' The journey, now about seventy miles by road, took him fourteen weeks 'in a bitter Winter Season not knowing what Bread or Bed did Mean.'[2]

Williams did not leave a detailed account of his travels in this period except to say that 'the ravens [that is, Native Americans] fed me in the wilderness.' He probably went south to Plymouth territory where he knew the Native Americans, in particular a sachem called Ousamequin (Massasoit). In *The Key* he recalled his afflictions in verse:

God makes a Path, provides a Guide,
And feeds in Wilderness!
His glorious Name while breath remains,
O that I may confess.

Lost many a time, I have had no Guide,
No House, but Hollow Tree!
In stormy Winter night no Fire,
No Food, no Company:

In him I have found a House, a Bed,
A Table, Company:
No Cup so bitter, but's made sweet,
When God shall Sweet'ning be.[3]

Writing a little later in 1670, he concluded:

The Lord is Righteous in all our Afflictions, that is a Maxim. The Lord is gracious to all oppressed, that is another. He is most gracious to the Soul that cries and waits on Him, that's Silver tried in the Fire 7 times.[4]

On reaching an area near Narragansett Bay he settled, and was soon joined by others from Salem, including one William Harris who would cause him great trouble. Some later accounts say he had company as he travelled, but he was adamant (writing in 1677) that 'it is not true that I was employed by any, made Covenant with any, or desired any to come with me into these parts.'[5] In his journal, Winthrop writes that Williams was part of a plan by Separatists earlier in 1635 to settle in the area. Cotton in his letter of reply to Williams in 1647 said, 'some of his friends went to the place appointed by himself beforehand.'[6] He had obviously made some plans, probably in the period after the banishment order in October 1635: he had mortgaged his house for example 'for Supplies;'[7] it was perhaps not the idea of leaving Salem, not even the prospect of being banished, but the sudden order of repatriation that took him by surprise.

He wrote in 1677 (and at other times) that 'My Soul's desire was to do the natives good and to that End learn their Language (which I afterward printed) and therefore desired not to be troubled with English Company.'[8] At least not straightaway. But he was. Within a year some thirty people had joined him, about twenty coming from his former congregation at Salem. After Williams left, Salem dissenters who held his views and wanted to separate to form a new church were threatened by the magistrates with excommunication, their conduct being seen in Boston as 'very offensive to the government here, and may no longer be suffered.' Several left to follow Williams.

In his first resting place, on the eastern shore of the Seekonk River, he and the others who joined him began planting crops and building shelters for their families to follow. Before long Massachusetts was making its influence felt again. Williams received a courteous but firm letter from Edward Winslow, governor of Plymouth, asking him to move as they were trespassing on Plymouth territory, and Plymouth was 'loth to displease the Bay.' Williams and his group crossed the river, and in April 1636 landed at Slate Rock. So began the settlement that would become Providence and the state that would be Rhode Island, the lands surrounding Narragansett Bay and Aquidneck Island. The seal of the City of Providence pictures Roger Williams landing and the words 'What Cheer?' as his first greeting to waiting Native Americans was supposed to have been 'What Cheare, Netop [friend]?' Despite yet another complaint against their settlement, William Bradford, now Plymouth governor, wrote that Williams 'should not be molested and tossed up and down again while they had Breath in their Bodies.'[9]

Williams had to live. He had lost his trading with Native Americans and English on leaving Salem, and had lost his harvest on having to cross the river. He was destitute and was grateful for a kindly visit from Edward Winslow who 'put a piece of Gold' into his wife's hand. He was in Narragansett country and their sachem was the aged Canonicus whom Williams referred to as 'that old Prince' and who was 'most shy of all English to his last breath.' From Canonicus and his nephew Miantonomu, whom Canonicus allowed to exercise considerable power, Williams bought land— or at least he gave what he called 'gratuities' for it. The old chief would never have sold land to the English for mere money said Williams, but God had given Williams a 'Painful, Patient spirit to lodge with them in their filthy smokey holes (even while I lived at Plymouth and Salem) to gain their Tongue.'[10] The land was 'obtained by Love.'[11] On this land Providence was built, named for the many 'providences of the most holy and only wise.'

Williams purchased the land in his own name. A rather tattered deed of 1638 (two years later), formally recording this, bearing the marks of Canonicus (a bow) and Miantonomu (an arrow), can be seen in Rhode Island State House in Providence. He then assigned it to other individuals. The 'purchasers' enjoyed equal rights of voting and government. In later years Williams wrote that he had always stood for 'liberty and equality, both in land and government.' Six men, including Williams, were the original purchasers. Thirteen men, including Williams, signed an 'Initial Deed' in 1638 that consolidated previous transactions. Subsequent purchasers paid thirty shillings to Williams for their shares; once he was reimbursed his expenses he donated all his remaining land to the town of Providence and purchasers paid their thirty shillings into a 'town stock' (a common fund). Despite Williams' liberality and best efforts, however, disputes about ownership were to dog the colony for decades, not least around land at Pawtuxet, and the main antagonist of Williams was William Harris. Massachusetts meanwhile passed a law virtually prohibiting residents of Providence from entering the Bay's territory.

In the months that followed numbers grew. More came from Salem. By the end of 1638 the town population was eighty-five. A small but growing colony also needed government. At first this was by heads of households meeting fortnightly but this could not last as Providence grew. The first settlers agreed that 'the place should be for such as were destitute (especially for Conscience).'[12] But what form should government take? Massachusetts at least had a charter to guide them, as well as Winthrop's vision of a city on a hill. Williams had no documents, no resources other than what he had picked up in Massachusetts and his own experience. His own experience however included several years working with Sir Edward Coke. His own guiding light too was at least as clear, though quite different, from that of Winthrop. It was that Providence and Rhode Island should be 'a shelter for persons distressed for conscience.'[13] Ola Winslow comments, 'Stronger than any other principle underneath the structure of early Providence government was the hatred of oppression and the militant resentment of meddling with personal freedom in any form.'[14] 'At their first coming thither,' wrote John Winthrop, 'Mr Williams and the rest did make an order, that no man should be molested for his conscience.'[15] One of Williams' early biographers, James D. Knowles, asserted that he, 'chose to found his colony on pure democratic principles; as a commonwealth, where all civil power should be exercised by the people alone, and where

God should be the only ruler over the conscience.'[16] However difficult it was in practice to attain them, three principles guided Williams: liberty of conscience; separation of church and state; and government by the people, not by an oligarchy.

Williams was not the first Englishman in the area. A little to the north William Blackstone had escaped the Lord Brethren as well as the Lord Bishops and lived in splendid isolation. Isolation was not Williams' goal, even though he could have done without Englishmen for the time being. His life had been busy, full of people, and he confessed, even if reluctantly, that 'I desire not to sleep in security and dream of a Nest which no hand can reach. I cannot but expect changes, and the change of the last enemy, Death.' He added, 'I dare not despise a Liberty, which the Lord seems to offer me if for mine own or others' peace.'[17]

Changes came in the form of 'Young men single persons (of whom we had much need)' who arrived, 'discontented with their estate, and seek the "Freedom of Vote also, and equality."' Some form of constitution was needed. Williams wrote for advice to Winthrop, his anxiety about the 'young men' showing that he was not at this stage a democrat in the modern sense. He proposed two draft forms of incorporation, one for the householders, one for the 'young men,' but in August 1638 the town was incorporated and the following covenant was signed:

> We whose names are hereunder, desirous to inhabit in the town of Providence, do promise to subject ourselves in active or passive obedience to all such orders or agreements as shall be made for the public good of the body in an orderly way, by the major consent of the present inhabitants, masters of families, incorporated together into a Towne fellowship, and others whom they shall admit unto them, only in civil things.[18]

In July 1640, a more elaborate covenant called 'The Combination' was signed. The second article states, 'As formerly hath been the liberties of the Town: so Still to hold forth Liberty of Conscience.' It laid a broader basis for democratic government, the 'young single men' and substantially all townsmen became freemen at once with full rights to land.

Here then is a form of democracy, but two things are striking: first, obedience is promised in civil things only. That is, the government did not have the right to make, and inhabitants did not promise to observe, any legislation or other regulation concerning the religious life of residents. Subsequent covenants repeated this basic principle. Second, there is no mention of God. John Barry calls this 'extraordinary,' pointing out that all comparable founding documents began with explicit recognition of God such as, for example, Plymouth's Mayflower Compact, 'Having undertaken for the Glory of God, and Advancement of the Christian Faith.'[19]

Was this because Williams was not a religious man? Not at all. Nor would it have been because he did not exercise influence over the final wording of the covenant. His letters seep religion from every pore. Even by Puritan standards, the references in his letters to God, the Bible and seeing his life in spiritual terms, are prolific. He was a man whose every thought was related to God's Word, God's will and the pursuit of pure living and true worship. When it came to the state, however, it was clear that certain thoughts were developing. One was the relation of God to the state. To acknowledge God as the God of a *particular* state was illicitly appropriating a relation to God that could only be enjoyed by ancient Israel. In 1637 he sent a thirty-eight page manuscript, now lost, to two New England ministers at their request, showing the difference between Israel and all other states. He would develop this in the future. Further, no man should be oppressed in conscience. Williams had no doubt about God's existence, power and authority, but belief in him should not be imposed on human consciences, which was precisely what he saw and hated in Christendom—old Europe and now, as he saw it through painful experience, New England. The terms Christian or Christendom could not properly be applied to a nation, he wrote later; only the church is comprised of the people of God. Williams had no place for the supposedly Christian state which in reality was not Christian at all, and even less Christian in practice than many unbelievers (for Williams this meant the Native Americans) who lived under it. A king or nation that justified its actions solely by reference to the fact that they were Christians, were placing themselves on the same level as Catholic Antichrist.

One further element of the town's incorporation was that there was no power of veto for Williams—which he had actually asked Winthrop about in a letter (we do not have Winthrop's reply). Williams seems to have hoped that by virtue of his original ownership of the land and then his agreement to be bound by the majority vote, he might be entitled to exclude people he considered undesirable. But no such provision was made. Perhaps his conviction about the necessity of accepting change prevailed. In the end Rhode Island accepted not only troublesome young men, but compulsive troublemakers like Samuel Gorton, religious exiles like Anne Hutchinson and her followers and in due course numerous Quakers. Samuel Brockunier concludes that 'the Narragansett bay settlements were an embryo of the America that was to come.'[20]

Anne Hutchinson

After Roger Williams, Anne Hutchinson was the stiffest test the nascent colony of Massachusetts had to face. She was a woman of great brilliance and self-confidence. In England she had devotedly attended the preaching of John Cotton in Boston, Lincolnshire. Anne's brother-in-law John Wheelwright provided additional spiritual sustenance. In 1632 he was moved on, and John Cotton went to New England in 1633. Anne felt she must follow. With her husband William and their twelve children she arrived in Boston, Massachusetts in autumn 1634. She was appreciated as a midwife and nurse. What Anne liked about Cotton's preaching was the emphasis on the all-sufficient grace of God. Indeed, under his ministry the church in Boston knew something of a revival. Winthrop recorded his appreciation of Cotton's preaching. What can man contribute to his salvation? Nothing. It was all of grace. His preaching was in contrast to other New England ministers who emphasized 'preparationism' whereby the sinner was exhorted to use means to come to Christ by faith—self-examination in the light of God's law, grieving over sins, meditation and prayer.

Anne lapped up Cotton's teaching. She did more than that. She expanded on it. If works have nothing to do with one's conversion, then do they have anything to do with one's sanctification? Not only did Anne expand on Cotton's teaching, believing that she was doing no more than repeating it, she wanted to teach as well. She gathered a home group (not an unusual thing in itself); the group became eighty people, mostly but not exclusively women, and they had to move into the church. She began to accuse ministers who insisted on the moral law as bound in a 'covenant of works.' The new young governor Henry Vane became a follower. John Wheelwright arrived from England and Anne tried to get him appointed assistant teacher with Cotton in Boston. This would have pushed the pastor John Wilson even further into the background. Wheelwright went elsewhere—Winthrop helping to defeat the proposed appointment—but the church was split. John Cotton himself came under scrutiny. Ministers began to criticize him for 'advancing the Spirit,' trusting revelations of the Spirit, destroying confidence in the revelation of Scripture, and depending on Christ's righteousness to the exclusion of good works in any phase of the Christian life. The only evidence of salvation needed, argued Hutchinson, was the inner presence and work of the Spirit. Sanctification was no evidence of justification. In Edwin Gaustad's words, the bond between the new birth and morality was accidental, not essential.[21] She was, it seemed, an antinomian—one who believes that the law of God has little, or no, role to play in the life of a Christian. Moreover, though sanctification was no sure evidence of justification, she and her followers had no hesitation in pronouncing on the salvation of others, including the ministers she declared to be under a 'covenant of works,' that is, unsaved.

Boston had to act. Winthrop, a member of the church but not governor at this point, took the lead. He began compiling a list of dangerous propositions that could be deduced from her views—which is different from saying she held them. The list of errors came eventually to eighty-two. After a lecture by Cotton in January 1637 Wheelwright rose up to attack those who supposed sanctification was evidence of justification. They were under a covenant of works; 'the more holy they are, the greater enemies they are to Christ;' so true believers must hew them down; 'we must lay load upon them, we must kill them with the words of the Lord.' Metaphor indeed, but it could be misinterpreted.

A General Court meeting was held to appoint officers. Vane was voted off; Winthrop was governor again. He called a day of humiliation and fasting. He acted slowly and with restraint. Cotton refused to condemn Hutchinson, maintaining that she did not hold the heresies attributed to her. In addition he disapproved of the preparationist views held by many of the New England ministers. He sat on the fence. To prevent settlement of groups holding similar views (he had in mind particularly a sect called the Grindletonians in England) Winthrop sponsored the passing of an order forbidding anyone giving hospitality to strangers for more than three weeks without permission from the magistrates. But he gave, nonetheless, the friends and relatives of Hutchinson and Wheelwright four months to leave the colony.

In August 1637 the ministers met. For twenty-four days they debated their list of eighty-two heretical propositions. Wheelwright was banished by the General Court. Hutchinson was called to appear, the ministers on hand as witnesses. She acquitted herself well. The magistrates found it difficult to pin her down. What sounds heretical in a particular context can sound ambivalent, even perfectly orthodox, in another. The matter of dishonouring the ministers came up, and this was where the evidence was firmest. Had she said they were unsaved, under a covenant of works? Cotton appeared as witness. 'I must say,' he said, 'that I did not find her saying they were under a covenant of works, nor that she said they did preach a covenant of works.' The case against Hutchinson appeared to have collapsed. And then, perhaps hysterical, in the emotion of the occasion, she condemned herself. She poured forth what purported to be divine revelation, immediate revelation to her soul. That was enough. The Puritans referred to the Bible only for revelation. She was undermining their ultimate authority. She was banished. 'I desire to know wherefore I am banished,' she asked, not unreasonably. 'Say no more,' admonished Winthrop, 'the court knows wherefore and is satisfied.'

Anne Hutchinson went south—to Rhode Island. She settled at what became Portsmouth on Aquidneck Island. Later, after her husband's death, she moved with her younger children to the Dutch colony of New Amsterdam (New York). In 1643 she was killed in a Native American attack.

The case shows how Massachusetts worked. Without any doubt, Hutchinson's views were unorthodox by the canons of Reformed theology and the church should have disciplined her. We are less familiar with heresy being seen as a threat to the state. This is how her views were seen, however. It was not only because New England was young and insecure. Views such as hers would have been punished in any Christian country. She raised the spectre of sixteenth century Anabaptism, with its 'enthusiasm,' antinomian moral licence and claims to personal revelation.

Her case reveals how similar New England was to the rest of Christendom. No question was raised about whether the magistrates should have been trying a church member for heresy. In Williams' case, church, represented by the ministers, always on hand to advise the magistrates, and state, were close. Hutchinson's was very obviously a religious case; Williams' was more ambiguous though his objection to the oath, to magistrates' jurisdiction over matters of personal worship, and to the king's grant of the land, were in that age very obviously threats to the civil sphere. Yet the letter to the churches, the rebuke for not reading it and the call for Salem to separate, were church issues. These were probably the last straw for the Boston magistrates and ministers. But in the end both dissidents would threaten both state and church where those institutions were too closely entwined and interdependent.

Both, too, threatened the authority of the ministers and magistrates. Williams was condemned for broaching dangerous opinions 'against the authority of magistrates;' Hutchinson could not be bested in debate but she was setting forward and adhering to her opinions, 'and so you do dishonour us,' said an exasperated Winthrop at her trial. According to Cotton Mather, drawing on John Winthrop, a testimony from heaven against the sectaries came when Anne Hutchinson was 'delivered of about thirty monstrous births at once,' and another, (Mary Dyer, later a Quaker) was recorded in October 1637 as being, 'delivered of as

hideous a monster as perhaps the sun ever lookt upon'—claws and
all—and the bed was shaken by an 'invisible hand.'[22]

Rhode Island was different. Radically different. This was not
because the residents (still a fairly small group at this time)
necessarily agreed with her views. Some may have, some may not.
Williams certainly did not. There was no man more committed
to the literal word of Scripture, less inclined to claim personal
revelation, as his later debates with Quakers showed. No-one,
despite all the accusations made against him for 'dangerous
opinions' and his evident particularity on minor issues (as we
would see them), ever accused Williams of serious theological
heresy. He was adjudged, by 'many judicious persons,' to have
had, 'the root of the matter in him,' concluded Cotton Mather.[23]
The difference was that Rhode Island was committed from
the outset to being a refuge for those distressed, 'especially for
conscience,' where human beings could live in society even if they
disagreed over religion. This was unprecedented in the known
world at that time, certainly in old Christendom, and also in New
England. It would prove, though, to be the way forward; to be the
only way New England itself could survive.

John Cotton's part in the furore shows a certain ambivalence. At
first he was supportive of Anne Hutchinson's meetings. He said
though that he did warn her of the danger of 'private meditations
or revelations only.' But there was a difference between him and
other ministers. For men such as John Wilson the first evidence of
justification was good works or sanctification; for Cotton, it was
an awareness of the presence of the Spirit. It was an overemphasis
on this element of her pastor's teaching that Hutchinson
taught. Her teaching promoted a radical individualism, a kind
of Gnosticism even; it severed the much-desired unity in both
church and society; it removed her and her followers from any
kind of pastoral or magisterial control—for who can gainsay

one to whom God speaks directly? Cotton was in a difficult position; two-thirds of his church and most of the church officers supported Hutchinson. Cotton was not as extreme as Hutchinson, his wayward disciple, but his views did create suspicion amongst, indeed serious opposition from, his fellow ministers. He survived by holding to his original position but in more measured terms than Hutchinson.

Helping Massachusetts

The early days in Providence witnessed a new development in the relationship between Williams and his former home. He was useful to Massachusetts time and again as a negotiator with Native Americans. The Narragansetts were the dominant tribe in the area and soon after Williams arrived he helped to defuse 'a great contest' between them and the Wampanoags, his old friends in the Plymouth area whose chief Massasoit, with others, had helped him through the snow. He wrote of this time that Miantonomu enjoyed visiting him and 'kept his barbarous court lately at my house.'

An altogether more serious incident was sparked later in 1636 when a Massachusetts trader, John Oldham, was killed on Block Island, off the south coast of Rhode Island, by Pequots. Massachusetts sent a punitive expedition that destroyed a Pequot settlement. This only enraged the Pequots further and soon it was clear that war was inevitable. Williams' achievement was to prevent an alliance, potentially disastrous for the English in New England, of Narragansetts with Pequots. At Boston's request the useful exile rushed to the Narragansett chief's house 'in a poor Canoe' cutting through a 'stormy Wind 30 mile in great seas every minute in hazard of Life' and then lodging with 'the bloody Pequot Ambassadors, whose Hands and Arms (me thought) wreaked with blood of my Countrymen murdered and massacred by them on

Connecticut River, and from whom I could not but nightly look for their bloody Knives at my own throat also.'[24]

His courage in negotiating not with the relatively friendly Narragansetts (though they too were angered by English aggression and later by a plague they blamed on the English) but with the bloodthirsty Pequots, one white man among a thousand Natives plotting war against the whites, commands respect. His skill as a negotiator saved the day insofar as the alliance of the two tribes was prevented. In May 1637 the 'English were ready to fight the Pequots. Williams gave advice on the manoeuvres and location of the Pequots and on how best to engage them. The Narragansetts had asked that women and children be spared. Canonicus the old Narragansett chief asked for a box of sugar for his compliance. Williams and he were dismayed when the English (a force made up from Boston, Connecticut and Plymouth) burned down a fort killing all 500 inhabitants. It was the end of the Pequot tribe. The few survivors became slaves—the first in New England, but not the last. Williams himself received one boy whom he treated well as the boy stayed with him rather than return to his mother.[25] 'I fear some innocent blood cries at Connecticut,' he wrote to Winthrop in July 1637, citing 2 Kings 14:5–6—children should not be put to death for their fathers' sins and vice versa.[26] Murderers deserved vengeance—but not the whole tribe.

As thanks for his help Winthrop proposed that Williams be recalled from banishment, and honoured with 'some Remark of Favour.' It was opposed. Too many in Boston feared him.

Chapter 7

Church in Rhode Island?

THERE WAS NO CRITERION OF CHURCH MEMBERSHIP FOR POLITICAL suffrage in Providence. Then again, there was no church. Not for half a century was there a church building. In most New England towns building a church would be among the first projects. The houses in Providence were laid out in a straight line, not around a town common with a church. People worshipped in their homes. Williams seemed to have gone from the sacred public square to the naked public square in one step.[1]

In 1639 Williams joined twenty others and formed the first Baptist church in America. He had himself baptized (or re-baptized, as Massachusetts would have said) by Ezekiel Holliman, another reject from Salem. In 1639 Salem church passed a 'great censure' (Williams called it a 'bull of excommunication') on those of its former members who were re-baptized at Providence.

Williams had read Baptist writings and warmed to their rejection of state authority over belief and worship. W. Clark

Gilpin points out, for instance, the similarity between Helwys'
The Mystery of Iniquity and Williams' thinking.[2] Adherence to
proper forms of outward worship was important to Williams
(unlike to some Separatists); even nominal connection with the
Church of England was spiritually damaging; and only those who
had separated themselves from such pollutions were qualified to
form authentic churches. These Baptists were 'Particular' in that
they were Calvinistic in theology. Even that was not enough to
keep Williams among them. Within a few months he had left the
church. He was never to be a member of a church again.

At this point those hostile to Williams shake their heads
and say, 'Told you so.' There was much head shaking in
Massachusetts. Those with any lingering sympathy for him
find it in imminent danger of evaporating. 'Why, Roger—don't
you know when to stop?' we groan. Winthrop and others put it
down to conversations with the antinomians and especially with
Anne Hutchinson's sister Catherine Scott who had settled in
Portsmouth. Williams would only worship with his wife, wrote
Winthrop, but there is no other evidence of that assertion.

Had he lost his faith? Not at all. His reasons for leaving not
only the Baptist church in Providence but all churches were
profoundly, if to us mysteriously, theological. It boils down to the
belief that no valid church could be established without an apostle;
that in the dark and apostate years of the post-Constantinian
settlement the true church had disappeared; and that there was
no-one now with the authority to establish a church. It is not that
he had rejected the idea of church; it is just that he did not know
where to find a true church on earth. How had he come to this
conviction?

Awaiting the millennium
Puritans in the 1630s and 1640s were great preachers, pastors and

theologians who cared for souls and developed Christian theology to a pinnacle of excellence. They were also profoundly concerned about doing God's will on earth, sanctifying not only individual souls but the nation, and tracing God's hand in history and their own day. They believed that they were living in a decisive moment in history, perhaps even the final age, during which God was reforming the church out of the corruption into which she had fallen in the Middle Ages.

Their thinking about both eternal blessedness and the earthly reign of God was evident in and influenced by their contemplations on the millennium, the period of 1,000 years prophesied in Revelation 20. The predominant interpretation since Augustine in the fifth century was that this period was symbolic of the whole church age. The view that it was a period of a literal 1,000 years in which Christ reigned physically on earth with his saints was condemned. In the seventeenth century, however, the view that the millennium was a literal period of prosperity for the church became very popular and with it the recovery (though among Puritans only ever a minority position) of the idea that Christ would return and reign over the earth with his saints for the millennium before his final appearing and judgement. Today we would call this view premillennialism. The idea of a glorious period *before* his return is called postmillennialism; Augustine's view of the millennium as the whole church age is now called amillennialism. In the sixteenth and seventeenth centuries these distinctions were present but not so labelled. What was powerful among Puritans was the idea of an age of glory for the church to come and in the light of such thinking their own lives and political events were fraught with historical significance. To understand Roger Williams it is necessary to look at this.

John Foxe in his *Book of Martyrs* had popularized the idea of

England re-enacting the role of ancient Israel as a people in special covenant with God. The reconstruction of history along Protestant lines was hugely important over the next century. Foxe divided history into five ages, the first being the age of suffering, the second, third and fourth comprising the millennium, beginning with the flourishing time of Constantine but ending in the darkness of papal supremacy. The fifth period began with reformers Wycliffe and Huss in the fourteenth and fifteenth centuries and was a time of reformation in which Foxe of course lived. The true church, led by England under her Protestant queen, was locked in battle with the forces of Antichrist (the papacy) making way for the return of Christ, potentially at any time.

Two other learned scholars greatly influenced the Puritans. Thomas Brightman (1562–1607) saw the course of history laid out in the book of Revelation and the millennium ending about 1300 but then a second millennium began, the Reformation marking the beginning of the saints' reign with Christ. During these final thousand years of history the church would experience a glorious purity made possible by Christian magistrates, through whom Christ would exercise his lordship so that they would 'give themselves wholly to seek the advancing of his glory.' Pre-eminent among these godly sovereigns was Elizabeth herself. The Pope was Antichrist. Christ would return in the year 2300 and translate his kingdom to heaven. The latter half of the seventeenth century was to see cataclysmic changes, seeing the conversion of the Jews and the destruction of Christ's enemies.

The second influential scholar was Joseph Mede (1586–1638), a conforming scholar at Cambridge, and his influence shows that interest in the millennium was not exclusive to Puritans. Writing during the Thirty Years' War in 1627, Mede was wary of seeing the course of world history in Revelation and was less optimistic than Brightman. Indulging less in calculations, Mede was more concerned with developing a critical method for interpreting the symbols and visions of the book. He saw two principle prophecies, in Revelation chapters 4–11 and chapters 12–21, and placed the tribulations just prior to the advent of the millennium. He saw the slaughter of the witnesses in Revelation 11:7 as yet to come, whereas Brightman believed it had already happened. Therefore Mede's millennium was in the future and would mean Christ's reign with his saints. Here was full-blown 'chiliasm' or millenarianism—what is now called premillennialism.

Among Puritans the themes of the role of England in world history, the defeat of Antichrist (the Pope), the conversion of the Jews, the conversion of the nations, the importance of purifying the church and personal piety, recur. Those with millenarian tendencies included William Twisse, Jeremiah Burroughs, William Bridge and Thomas Goodwin. Goodwin interpreted Revelation to give an exact chronology of history from the end of the first century. Reforming church government (along Independent or Congregational lines) was part of purifying the church for the millennium. He believed that the millennium would begin in or just before the year 1700 when Christ and 'part of heaven shall come down and rule this world.'

Millenarianism was unpopular in Scotland and among Presbyterians generally. The extreme face of chiliasm was the Fifth Monarchy Men who believed that the eternal kingdom and the reign of the saints (the millennium) after the destruction of the four kingdoms in Daniel 7, was to begin on the death of Charles 1. Men like Goodwin distanced themselves from these groups. Revelation 11—the death of the two witnesses—was an important text, for it suggested the final suffering of the church and also its imminent resurrection—but were these events past, present or future?

Inevitably these trends affected the Puritans in New England. Millennial thinking was not in itself the motive for the migration to New England, but John Cotton, John Eliot, Thomas Hooker and others were optimistic about the millennium; Eliot was strongly motivated in his missionary work among the Native Americans by the desire to prepare for the return of Christ. He published a premillennial work in the 1650s but retracted it after the restoration of the monarchy in 1660. The Puritans were looking for a present-day promised land, a New Jerusalem. There was heightened millennial speculation around 1640; Cotton preached three series of sermons on Revelation between 1639 and 1641. In the period of the Puritans' greatest optimism, the mid-1640s, Cotton wrote that he believed the millennium would begin in the next decade. George Gillespie, a Scottish Presbyterian Commissioner to the Westminster Assembly, used Ezekiel 43:11 to preach before Parliament in 1644 that Christ would return at the end of the millennium, predicting a 'more glorious Church in the latter days,' and that this golden age was imminent. Parliament should see itself as God's agent in bringing in the millennium.

The congregational system adopted in New England placed a premium on church purity, a preparation for the millennial kingdom. Cotton, with others following him, applied 'admission tests,' such as asking for an account of their conversion experience, to prospective members to seek to ensure church purity. Yet the 'mainline' ministers in New England were prepared to pursue purity without turning their backs completely on the Church of England. They were happy to say they were separating from the corruptions of the Church but not from the Church itself.

To 'the left' were churches, like Salem, who insisted on a covenant between believing Christians as the basis of a church. This was similar to the position of those in England like the Henry Jacob church in London which operated as a 'church within the

Church' and insisted they were not Separatists. Salem's objection to offering the sacraments to the Winthrop settlers was that they were not members of any particular reformed church. By denying that an explicit congregational covenant was of the essence of the church (although it could be an aid to sanctification) Cotton, however, enabled himself to stay within the Church of England yet seek its reform. This position, as we shall see, only drew undiluted scorn from Williams. Cotton said he was mediating between two extremes; Williams said he was halting between two opinions. How can you promise loyalty to an institution you think is corrupt and needs reform?

Further to the left of the Church of England were Separatists like John Robinson in Leiden and the Plymouth settlers. But they did not denounce it, allowing members to listen to sermons and not repudiating the Church of England as a false church.

Yet further left were true Separatists like Henry Barrowe in the sixteenth century and Williams' contemporary John Canne who objected to three things in the Church of England: its worship, which was contaminated by 'popish trumperies,' its parish system, which mixed the godly with the profane in worship and membership and its government, with bishops also acting as officials of state. That church was therefore to be repudiated.

Further to the left still was Roger Williams. In England he had made it clear he 'durst not' join with any who worshipped with the Book of Common Prayer. This was a standard Separatist position—such written liturgy stifled the Spirit. To the congregational way of admitting members in New England he would have added, as a qualification for membership, repentance for and repudiation of former association with the Church of England. True piety involved the outward observances of worship and was not just a state of mind. Puritans who stayed within the Church were forgetting that. Scrupulous attention to external details in worship was not legalism but was necessary evidence of a right heart that sought pure worship. The piety of the individual and of the congregation could only be preserved and advanced by cutting oneself off from the corrupt church. Moreover, Puritans recognised that it was not right to be indiscriminate in administering the Lord's Supper. Why then was it permissible to be indiscriminate in hearing preaching? Was it not as much part of worship as the sacrament? Preaching, for Williams, was not apostolically authorized to be for conversion, but was a ministry to the saints.

In this stance, Williams would have said, he was not being untrue to the principles of the Puritans themselves. He and other radical Separatists were simply taking those principles to their logical conclusion.

To these Separatist principles Williams added a distinctive form of millenarianism.[3] Here again, though, he was not completely novel in his views; he was just at the extreme end of a spectrum. It was all about the quest for the true church; ultimately for the perfect church which will come when Christ returns. What caused Williams to think that a true church (not the perfect church) could not be found on earth?

At some point Williams became convinced that a church was not formed by covenant (the conventional congregational view in New England) but by apostolic ministers commissioned by Christ. The only such apostles were the original twelve or those who could trace their authority by succession back to them and therefore to Christ himself. This succession of ministers however was broken by the corruption of the medieval church and Christians were left without the means of forming themselves into congregations or administering sacraments. Only at the millennium (which Williams at this time believed to be close at hand) would true apostles be appointed again by Christ. Until then Williams could not in conscience take the sacrament or be a church member. He had replaced both covenant and believers' baptism with a form of apostolic succession as the foundation of a church.

Like many Puritans, Williams believed the church was emerging out of the reign of Antichrist (broadly speaking the Middle Ages) but he was more pessimistic about the impact that period had had on the church. It had been 'put to flight,' he said, 'and retired into the Wilderness of Desolation.'[4] Neither 'the begetting ministry of the apostles or messengers to the nations, or the feeding ministry of pastors and teachers, according to the first institution of the Lord Jesus, are yet restored and extant.'[5] Yet God had not left himself without witness and through prophets and witnesses 'in sackcloth' (a reference to Revelation 11:3) such as the Waldensians, followers of Wycliffe and Huss, Luther and Calvin, God still spoke. Such witnesses or prophets were probably, according to this line of thinking, identical with the 144,000 Virgins, mystical Israel, standing with the Lamb on Mount Zion (in Revelation 7)—they would reign in the millennial church, Christ having come first—what we would call a premillennial view.[6] The task of such prophets in sackcloth was not to form churches but to continue a witness against Antichrist and the corruption of the church.

Williams therefore identified himself with what we might call the 'pilgrim church,' as a witness for God and for truth in a corrupt generation, in which there was no biblical authority to form a church, but only to witness as a warning to the false church and a call to repentance. He did not believe this state of affairs would last for long—the nations would soon be enraged by their witness and, following Revelation 11, they would be killed, only to rise again, and see the success of the church. The coming glory would bring true apostles again and the true church, restored to its primitive New Testament pattern. 'Christ's witnesses must purge the church before Christ's apostles rebuild it,' was his view.[7] For the time being, external acts such as the sacraments could not properly be the expression of true worship or means of grace; in the future age they would be, but now Christians were deprived of being able to express their faith through the ordained channels. Prophets in sackcloth could meet for fellowship and to be encouraged by preaching, but they would not constitute a church.

Where did Williams get his millennial system? Williams was not as outlandish as we may think. John Owen, for example, also identified the period of Papal dominance with the wilderness years of the church in which God raised up witnesses in sackcloth, but he saw the church reviving during the ministry of the Reformers; Williams saw the Reformers themselves still as witnesses in sackcloth.[8] The complete loss of the visible church, however, the expected primitivism of the restored millennial church and the insistence on outward and visible ordinances (rather than the expected spiritual church envisaged by most Puritans) were barely discernible in other writings.

There had, however, been views among earlier Separatists and General Baptists such as Helwys and Murton of Christ's appointment of new apostles to restore the church. Separatists like Bartholomew Legate, John Wilkinson and more latterly Lodowicke Muggleton claimed to be the two witnesses of Revelation 11, or even the new apostles themselves. John Winthrop did, in 1639, express the view that Williams expected 'to become an apostle,' but there is no evidence in Williams' writings that he saw himself as other than one of a number of 'prophets in sackcloth' awaiting the new apostles. The reception of prophetic revelation or special experiences of the Spirit, particularly during times of suffering for their beliefs, were other characteristics of sectarians and 'enthusiasts' such as John Canne, John Saltmarsh and John Lilburne (leader of the Levellers), as well as Anne Hutchinson and her sister Catherine, both of whom Williams had conversed with in New England. It was perhaps Williams' education, worldly experience and earlier exposure to the Puritans of Cambridge and Essex that prevented him falling into similar extremes, though he is certainly on the fringe of these movements in the way he described his ministry and his sufferings in exile 'in the wilderness.'

Reflecting on Williams' views, James D. Knowles writes:

> We need not pause, now, to show that his views were erroneous. We must deeply regret, that he formed them. But we cannot doubt his sincerity ... His opinions appear to have rested entirely on a misconception of passages in the Revelations. He believed that the 'white troopers' mentioned in the 6th and 19th chapters ... were the true ministers, and that they had been utterly routed till after the slaying of the witnesses and their resurrection.[9]

Williams saw himself as a prophet in sackcloth. He never described himself as a Seeker, which is what others who held similar ideas about the church were labelled, and what Williams, not surprisingly, was called or a least associated with by Robert Baillie, the Westminster Assembly Commissioner, and Richard Baxter. Seekers however characteristically had a mystical bent and in some cases scepticism towards the authority of the Bible which were absent in Williams. Such was the intellectual ferment about the nature and form of the church in the 1640s however that Williams' views did not seem as outlandish as they might today; Cromwell and Milton also held views that suggest sympathies with Seeker ideas.

Some biographers have tried to adopt Williams into the fold of modern relativism by suggesting that he gave up on finding absolute truth, even in the Bible. This is quite false. Williams believed firmly that the Bible was the Word of God—his later debates, as we shall see, with the Quakers in Rhode Island proved that beyond doubt. He did not believe that ministers had apostolic authority to found churches; or that truly authorized churches existed on earth; but these (though to us strange) were *beliefs* not doubts. He was not a postmodern seeker after truth that is never to be found; and he was not a Seeker even in seventeenth century terms.

Despite his views on the church, Williams did meet with others for public worship on Lord's Day mornings and once a month for many years he went to hold services in Narragansett country. He was recorded in 1666 as preaching 'well and able, and much people comes to hear him to their good satisfaction.'[10] But for Williams such voluntary groups would not have been a true church. It was only the best possible in this age.

His view of the Sabbath was expressed in a letter of 1670, answering criticisms that Rhode Islanders were a profane people, not keeping the Sabbath but 'some do plough ... etc.'[11] He first pointed out that the orthodox did not keep the Sabbath 'which is the 7th day.' Clearly the first day of the week was not for him the Sabbath even if it was a day of rest and worship. He then refers approvingly to Calvin who, 'held it but Ceremonial and figurative (from Colossians 2 etc.) and vanished: and that the Day of Worship was alterable at the Churches pleasure ....' He continues, however, 'You know also that generally all this whole Colony observe the first day. Only here and there, one out of Conscience, another out of Covetousness make no Conscience of it.' Because of Rhode Island's dislike of 'forced worship' Sabbath observance was not made a law of the state. Williams was known to have objected to travelling on a Sunday, but to have traded with Native Americans and one Native American sachem told John Eliot that they did not care to learn from Williams 'because he is no good man but goes out and works upon the Sabbath day.'[12] In 1672 he was willing to debate with Quakers on the Sabbath but they put it off until the Monday. His friend John Clarke in Newport believed the Sabbath was ceremonial. In 1672 America's first Seventh Day Baptist church was founded in Newport.

Winton Solberg says that 'In the last half of the seventeenth century Rhode Island developed a pattern of Sabbatarianism resembling that of more orthodox colonies.'[13] Laws were passed to make the First Day (avoiding use of the words 'Lord's Day,' 'Sunday' or 'Sabbath') the rest day while protecting liberty of conscience and avoiding 'forced worship.' Gaming and tippling were forbidden. In 1679 employment of servants was prohibited on Sunday and further pastimes were prohibited. In 1750 fines for breaking the regulations were increased. There was a desire to protect the traditional Christian day of rest and worship while allowing for liberty of conscience. As Solberg says, 'A large degree of religious freedom prevailed in Rhode Island. Attendance at church was entirely a private matter and the "stink of forced worship" never arose in the colony.'

Where does one place Williams theologically? In terms of his basic system, his doctrines of God, of man, of Christ, of salvation, he was clearly Calvinistic. Calvinism is more than the famous 'five points' but those core doctrines of grace—total depravity, unconditional election, particular redemption, irresistible grace, the perseverance of the saints—were his firm beliefs. At times indeed there is a hint of hyper-Calvinism, in his assurance that the elect cannot be lost, virtually regardless of malign influences upon them. In his desire for purity in personal life and the church, in taking the Bible as God's Word with utmost seriousness and trying to bring every area of life under its direction and his dissatisfaction with the established church he was in disposition as well as doctrine a Puritan, though unlike the more mainstream Puritans he rejected an established church completely. In his eventual rejection of the possibility of all forms of a true earthly church he could be called a sectarian, though definitions vary.

Central for Williams was the incarnation. The coming of Christ was for him the major turning point in history. His strong typology led him to see Christ and the church as fulfilling Old Testament types, notably the nation of Israel. This sense of biblical continuity between promise and fulfilment led to a radical form of discontinuity—between the Old and New Testaments, to the extent that the Old, being fulfilled, was almost no longer necessary except for useful examples. Williams embraced discontinuity in other ways: between church and state (separation so far as possible); between creation (this fallen world) and redemption—the old and new creations (the old has little to contribute to the new); between the kingdoms of the world and the kingdom of God (earthly government has little to do with Christ's kingdom). He also maintained a strong contrast between conversion as regeneration (that is true, spiritual conversion) and spurious, coerced or merely external 'conversion.'

For Williams, too, the church was called to follow the incarnate, servant Saviour with appropriate meekness. This sat uncomfortably with the assumption that Christians were born to rule.

But a civil state had to be built nonetheless and Williams had plenty of work to do.

Chapter 8

A Charter

IN 1637, AT THE TIME OF THE HUTCHINSON CONTROVERSY, SAMUEL Gorton arrived in Boston. Edward Winslow of Plymouth called him a 'pestilent disturber of our societies.' He was a man born to fight, to let nothing pass, to cause trouble, though historian Samuel Brockunier asserts that his 'moral character was of the highest,' that he was not an anarchist but 'a champion of liberty in its larger sense and English to the core in his insistence on legal process and the rights of an Englishman.'[1]

He left Massachusetts for Plymouth and was banished from there for a variety of trouble-making encounters. He went to Portsmouth on Aquidneck Island, Rhode Island, where the Hutchinsonians had settled, and joined with them in opposing another prominent settler, William Coddington, who left to found the town of Newport on the south of the island. Gorton was soon showing contempt for authority, calling the magistrates ('justices') 'just asses,' and was banished. In 1641 he washed up at Providence with a small group of followers. His civil and religious views are summarized by Edwin Gaustad as, 'Emphasizing the full equality of the sexes, the full equality of family members, the equal right of all to govern, and the equal right of all to refuse to be governed,' with a contempt for all authority civil or ecclesiastical, and an emphasis on the indwelling Spirit in all believers in a way that prefigured the Quakers in later years. As Gaustad says, this 'made him a difficult member of any community.'[2] Williams wrote to Winthrop in March 1641 groaning that:

> Master Gorton, having foully abused high and low at Aquidneck is now bewitching and bemadding poor Providence, both with his unclean and foul censures of all the Ministers of this Country, (for which myself have in Christ's name withstood him) and also denying all visible and external Ordinances in depth of Familism.[3]

The 'Familists' were a sixteenth century German sect characterized by mysticism and rejection of authority and church structures. Gorton was not technically a member of such a group but it described him well enough. He was a powerful and attractive preacher who won many to his side.

Gorton got involved in existing disputes about land in Providence. 'The Combination' of 1640 had far from settled all disagreements and Gorton came as oil on troubled flames. There was particular unease about the exclusive holding of the land at Pawtuxet by the original proprietors in 1638. Eventually, to the relief of Williams and his supporters, Gorton and his followers left and established the town of Warwick a little further south. He and Williams seem to have enjoyed a better relationship after that, becoming political allies in protecting Rhode Island although always disagreeing about religion. Williams was never one to hold authority in contempt; he firmly believed in the need for civil authority in particular; and always stood steadfastly against any claims to the authority of 'inner light' over Scripture. Williams was being forced to confront the kind of anarchy that could result when people like Gorton or William Harris claimed 'reason of conscience' to justify any behaviour—as had one man, Joshua Verin, who forcibly restrained his wife from attending church. Williams knew the difference between freedom of conscience and libertarianism. He had to find ways of making it work in Rhode Island.

Meanwhile, a greater test of law and order was to come for the nascent colony. William Arnold who had supported Williams against Gorton, but only out of self-interest, fraudulently obtained title to the Pawtuxet land and, in 1642, with others submitted himself and the land to the jurisdiction of Massachusetts. Massachusetts accepted the invitation. The territorial integrity of Rhode Island was under threat. Plymouth and Connecticut began showing interest in claiming land in the Narragansett Bay area. It was time to appeal to the highest earthly authority. Rhode Island needed a charter, a patent. Roger Williams set off for England in early 1643. He had to go by way of New Amsterdam as Boston would not allow him passage. As he left harbour he saw the flames of the war that killed Anne Hutchinson.

London 1643–44

England had changed since Williams left in 1630. Charles and Laud had pushed forward their policy. The attempt to impose the Prayer Book on Scotland had led to the two Bishops' Wars in 1639–40 and left much of the north of England in Scottish hands. To raise money, in 1640 the impoverished Charles had to call Parliament. Three weeks later the uncooperative 'Short' Parliament was dissolved. Later that year the Long Parliament was convened. Sir Thomas Strafford was impeached and executed in 1641; Laud, already imprisoned, would be executed in 1645. In August 1642 Charles, now at Nottingham, declared war on Parliament. The Civil War had begun.

Into this cauldron two New England ministers, Thomas Weld

and Hugh Peter, came in 1641 to seek help from London. Hopeful for change in the mother country, many settlers had returned to England and the colony was struggling economically. These men were not in England to oppose Williams but they would not make his task any easier. Arriving in spring 1643 Williams found some things working against him, some for him. Against him was the low priority that a small territory like Rhode Island would have in light of the momentous political issues being contested in England. In his favour, however, was the new order and intellectual atmosphere. In England an environment was developing where everything could be questioned, and this suited Williams. Full freedom of conscience was as yet an aspiration of only a few but toleration was at least an issue aired openly. His friend Sir Henry Vane had proposed it in Parliament; the Scottish Presbyterian Robert Baillie, a Commissioner at the Westminster Assembly, said the word should not even be spoken. In Cromwell's army it was practised. Cromwell believed the free conscience made a better soldier. Even Baptists were becoming officers. Another friend of Williams, John Milton, would soon eloquently plead the case for freedom of the press and of publication in *Areopagitica.*

Williams also had friends in influential positions. As well as those just mentioned, Sir William Masham and Sir Thomas Barrington were still active in public life and Sir Robert Rich, Earl of Warwick, was, in November 1643, placed in charge of colonial affairs. Probably his greatest *entrée* into the new establishment however was the fruit of his own labours, his book *A Key into the Language of America.* Williams had used the weeks on the voyage from New England to prepare this manuscript for the press and it was published by Gregory Dexter, probably recommended to him by Milton, in September 1643. It was published at a time of great interest in Native American affairs in England. Not least, there was disappointment with the abject failure of New England, despite great trumpeting about taking the gospel to the Native Americans, to do anything about it. In a vigorous *apologia* for Massachusetts Bay, Weld and Peters could only boast of one known convert in fourteen years. More galling was the absence of any real effort. Robert Baillie, with some overstatement, said that 'only Williams in the time of his banishment from among them, did assay what could be done with those desolate souls, and by a little experience quickly did find a wonderful great facility to gain thousands of them.'[4]

The reign of Antichrist prospered as Catholic missionaries made converts, by whatever means; the return of Christ had to be preceded by the gospel reaching the nations, especially by the conversion of the Jews. If, as some believed, and as John Eliot (who began his preaching to the Native Americans in 1646) himself believed, the Native Americans were one of the lost tribes of Israel, their conversion was even more significant. Williams' book scratched where many were itching. It was the first of four he was to publish in England during this visit. This was not the first book dealing with Native American matters but it was the best and, for Williams, came at a propitious time.[5]

A Key into the Language of America
Its subtitle tells us that as well as a guide to the language of the natives of New England, it has observations on their customs, manners and worship and 'spiritual observations' of use to the English. Its contents were 'dearly bought in some few years hardship ... among the barbarians,' writes Williams. He explains that:

> There is a mixture of this Language North and South, from the place of my abode, about six hundred miles; yet within the two hundred miles [New England] their dialects do exceedingly differ; yet not so, but (within that compass) a man may, by this help,

converse with thousands of Natives all over the Country: and by such converse it may please the Father of Mercies to spread Civility, (and in his own most holy season) Christianity; for one Candle will light ten thousand, and it may please God to blesse a little Leaven to season the mighty Lump of those Peoples and Territories.[6]

In other words—he hoped his book would help the spread of the gospel.

A Key displays Williams' remarkable gift for observation as well as his facility with languages. He gives lists of vocabulary in sections—rather like a phrase book for the modern holidaymaker—such as salutation, eating and entertainment, sleep and lodging, travel, parts of the body, animals and birds, business and of course religion. They worshipped a great god but also many gods—elsewhere he says he discovered thirty-eight gods worshipped by them. He himself abstained from even watching their rituals which he calls 'Satan's Inventions and Worships.'[7] He frequently makes appreciative comments about their natural courtesy and kindness, especially to him in his wilderness exile from Salem:

I have known them leave their House and Mat
To lodge a Friend or stranger,
When Jewes and Christians oft have sent
Christ Jesus to the Manger

'Fore day they invocate their Gods,
though Many, False and New:
O how should that God worshipt be,
Who is but One and True?

They were persuaded that the God who made the English must be a greater god than their creator, because of all the riches the English have, but when told that 1,600 years earlier the English had been in their condition 'they are greatly affected with a secret hope concerning themselves.' Williams is keen to point out at any opportunity that as human beings, the Native Americans are every bit as good as the Europeans. The English might well find that 'Heaven open to Indians wild, but shut to thee.'

Williams was 'comfortably persuaded' that 'the Father of Spirits ... will in his holy season (I hope approaching) persuade these Gentiles of America to partake of the mercies of Europe.' Weld and Peters in London were saying that the Native Americans were not ready to receive Christ. Nor was John Cotton optimistic: he feared Williams' talk of 'such a conversion of the Indians was too hyperbolical,' and that 'though a form of Christian Religion may be professed amongst Christians with some facility: yet it is not so easy a matter to gain these Pagan Indians so much as to a form of our Religion.'[8]

Williams was the last man to risk spurious conversions. In 1645, in addition to his four books printed in 1643–44 (*A Key, Mr Cotton's Letter Examined and Answered, Queries of Highest Consideration* and *The Bloudy Tenent*), a pamphlet appeared that he must have left with the printers before leaving England.

Christenings Make Not Christians

Subtitled 'A Brief Discourse concerning the name *Heathen* commonly given to the Indians', the target of the work is the abuse of the name 'heathen' to imply wild, wicked or sub-human, 'dogs' who could be killed rather than risk the life of one 'Christian.' Williams' argument is that true Christians and the people of God in this age are the church of Christ; all other people are 'heathen.' In that case, he argues in what will be a favourite theme: there are many 'heathen' in so-called Christendom—or 'Christian' countries. As to the conversion of Native Americans, he writes, 'woe be to me if I call that conversion unto God, which is indeed a subversion of the soules of Millions in Christendome, from one false worship to another.' He evinces a revulsion against anything approaching forced conversion:

> [Jesus Christ] abhorres (as all men, yea the very Indians doe) an unwilling Spouse, and to enter into a forced bed: The will in worship, if true, is like a free vote ... JESUS CHRIST compells by the mighty persuasions of his Messengers to come in, but otherwise with earthly weapons he never did compell nor can be compelled.

He says that he could have brought thousands to a false conversion, to observance of the Lord's Day, to baptism, to a church service, to forms of prayer. Yet true conversion requires the preaching of the Word of God, a turning of the whole man from Satan to God, from idols to the living and true God.

He also said that he did not think the time for such conversion among the Native Americans was yet come. The 'great business' between Christ and Antichrist was not yet over, and Christ had yet, in his view, to send true preachers for this work. This theological orientation seems to have occurred after about 1638 for then he had written to Winthrop still hoping to win Native American souls; now he felt convinced their conversion could only take place in the millennial restoration.

John Eliot began his ministry among the Native Americans in 1646; there is nothing in Williams' writings to suggest that Eliot's labours changed his mind. Eliot's thinking too was strongly millennial. His desire was to contribute to the setting up of the kingdom of Christ, to see Christ reign over church and commonwealth, and he believed his Native American communities would be a manifestation of the millennium. Hugh Peter and John Cotton, although hoping for the approaching kingdom, were less optimistic about Native American conversion. Cotton wrote, 'till the seven plagues of the seven Angels be fulfilled

[Revelation 15:18], we cannot easily hope for the entrance of any New multitudes of men into the Church.'9

Williams was not alone in what we might call missional pessimism based on differing interpretations of Revelation. He differed from Puritans such as Eliot who believed in continuity between the institutions of this age and the coming kingdom, and that God was using the politics of the day to bring that kingdom in. He differed on the other hand from the likes of Sir Henry Vane, whose mysticism looked forward to a spiritual kingdom. Vane believed the 1260 years of the apostasy had destroyed the visible church; that the period had now nearly expired and a new age would come without religious forms; present religion was to enjoy Christ in his beauty in 'the secret chambers of his presence.' Williams on the other hand believed that this era of the wilderness was a transitional state between the apostolic churches and the approaching restoration. Within this epoch he had a definite task as a witness in sackcloth, but had no authority to convert Native Americans or minister to churches. True churches did not exist. He awaited the church's revival by Christ. Paradoxically, he did continue to minister among the Native Americans. What he could do he would—even if he believed he had not apostolic, converting, church-founding authority, he could witness to the truth.

In *Christenings* Williams was making a number of points: respectful treatment of the Native Americans; the need for conversions to be genuine; but above all he was firing another salvo in his war against the concept of Christendom whereby the name Christian, he was convinced, was being formalized and trivialized. A nation could not be 'Christian' in any meaningful sense; when John Cotton mocked Rhode Island by saying moving there from Massachusetts was moving from 'church to no church' he was almost Roman Catholic: equating a geographical entity, a territory, with the covenantal presence of God. Israel might justifiably have done that; no state since could. Nor should any nation as such be dismissed as heathen in distinction from those supposedly Christian; the line between true heathen and true Christian was very differently drawn and much closer, uncomfortably close, to home. His *A Key* and *Christenings* are in fact as much about seeking the true conversion of the English as of the Native Americans.

In New England meanwhile the four colonies, Massachusetts, Connecticut, Plymouth and New Haven, had joined in May 1643 in a military alliance (the 'United Colonies'), covenanting with the aim 'to advance the kingdom of our Lord Jesus Christ,' and to defend themselves against the Native Americans who, having heard of the 'distractions' in England, took the opportunity to cause trouble. Pointedly, Rhode Island was excluded—not being of the same 'nation and religion' presumably. Williams' friend Miantonomu, suspected of plotting against the English, was executed by Massachusetts (though they used a Native American to strike the blow). Samuel Gorton caused trouble and after an armed skirmish was detained in irons at Charlestown.

In London, Weld and Peters decided to stay, having been persuaded to strengthen the Parliamentary cause. Williams and his brothers Sydrach and Robert wrangled over their mother's estate but did not fall out. He also helped the poor of London obtain wood during a hard winter, as the king controlled the coal supply from Newcastle. Parliament made Robert Rich governor of American Plantations. Weld made Williams' task in relation to the charter more difficult by obtaining signatures to a document purporting to be a patent swallowing up Rhode Island territory into Massachusetts.

His task was made yet more difficult by the hardening of views against toleration. In late 1643, however, an old letter of John Cotton to Williams appeared in print in London. No-one quite knows who was responsible for its appearance. Cotton had written it to Williams in 1636 when Williams was toiling through the winter from Salem. Williams replied in February 1644 with *Mr Cottons Letter lately Printed, Examined and Answered.* He wrote of being denied the 'common aire' of Massachusetts and being 'exposed to winter miseries in a howling wilderness.' The problem? Church and state in Massachusetts were too closely entwined; banishment from one necessarily meant banishment from the other. The true church was a beautiful garden; the world was a wilderness:

> When they have opened a gap in the hedge or wall of Separation between the Garden of the Church and the Wilderness of the world, God hath ever broke down the wall itself, removed the Candlestick ... and made his Garden a Wilderness, as at this day.[10]

Mixing the church and the state corrupted the church.

Those with influence had heard of Gorton's imprisonment in Massachusetts, his narrow avoidance of the death sentence (only by virtue of the deputies outnumbering the magistrates in the Boston court) and the refusal to let him appeal to England.[11] Things were moving Williams' way. Henry Vane was as ever a moving spirit. On 14 March 1644, the charter was granted. The residents of Rhode Island (who were variously called 'scumme' and 'riff-raff,' their colony a 'sewer' and a 'latrina,') were addressed by Parliament as our 'well Affected and Industrious English,' and the combination of Providence, Portsmouth, and Newport were named 'Providence Plantations in the Narragansett Bay.'[12] Not until 1662 would the name officially become 'Rhode Island and Providence Plantations'—now, as then, the smallest state with the longest name. The charter gave the colony:

> Full Power and Authority to Govern and rule themselves, and such others as shall hereafter Inhabit within any part of the said Tract of

land, by such a form of Civil Government, as by voluntary consent
of all, or the greater Part of them shall find most suitable to their
Estates and Conditions.

The proviso was that Rhode Island's laws must be 'conformable
to the laws of England' so far as local circumstances allowed.

Permitting the 'greater Part' to establish laws made for an
explicitly democratic government. Decisions about religion were
left to the majority, knowing that Rhode Islanders wanted to leave
issues of religion out of the state's reach. Williams had succeeded.
Providence Plantations exceeded any other known state in the
world in its freedoms.

Williams was almost done in London for now—but not quite. In
summer 1643, Parliament had set up the Westminster Assembly
to advise it on reforming the Church of England. The idea of
a national church was assumed. The prestige of John Cotton
and Thomas Hooker was rewarded by their appointment as
members but they never attended. Presbyterians dominated; five
'Independents' or 'Congregationalists' led the argument for at
least toleration for Independency in the overwhelming movement
towards a Presbyterian church order along Scottish lines. Bishops
were abolished but Independents feared, with John Milton, that
'new presbyter' would be 'old Priest writ large.'

These Independents published *An Apologeticall Narration* early
in 1644 to make their position clear. They saw the millennium
coming and the recovery of independent church polity was a sign
of it. They wanted a middle way between Presbyterianism and the
chaos as they saw it of sectarianism, so distanced themselves from
Separatists. They were taking some steps towards toleration but
not steps big enough for the likes of Henry Vane, John Milton or
Roger Williams. The Independents stressed the responsibilities
of magistrates in protecting and purifying the church—anathema

to Williams. Williams wanted freedom. Toleration smacked of a licence granted from on high which assumed the superiority of the grantor and could be withdrawn at will; freedom assumed the equality and rights of human beings to be able, in religious affairs at least, to hold and pursue their own beliefs. He wrote what would be the third in sequence of his works to be published in London.

Queries of Highest Consideration

This pamphlet was published anonymously; no licence would have been granted for it. Dexter, at considerable risk, printed it. Williams first challenged government censorship:

> It is a woeful privilege attending all great states and personages that they seldom hear any other music but what is known will please them ... who can pass the many locks and bars of any of the several licensers appointed by you? ... it is rarely possible that any other light ... shall ever shine on your Honours' souls, though ne'er so sweet, so necessary, and though it come from God.

He then addressed twelve questions to the five dissenting (Independent) brethren and to the Scottish Commissioners appointed to the Assembly. His first query was indeed high. By what authority did the Assembly sit? Such questions cause strong men to grab tin hats and dive for the trenches. If the answer is Acts 15 (as many claimed) then—does a modern state have the authority of the ancient apostles? Query two asked what authority a state-sponsored institution had to define worship for the people of God. For Williams, a government was appointed by the people; it had no more authority (and none anyway in relation to the church) than the people could bestow. Would the world determine what the church of Christ was to believe and how it was to worship? Church discipline was the responsibility of the church alone. He disagreed with the Independents and Presbyterians that Parliament should be an agent of church reform.

Williams, it must be made clear, did not disagree with the Westminster divines on the vast majority of their doctrine, on the great issues of Scripture, God, Christ and salvation; but it was not for a state to impose it. What if Henry VIII had called such an Assembly? Or Edward VI? Or Mary? Elizabeth? James? And just what had Charles and Laud been trying to do? This was a return to the High Commission; to Moses. If a state froze Christian worship at any given time—look how many different versions of Christianity might have been imposed! The fact that one's theology may be a lot more correct did not change the basic principle: religion should not be imposed by a national government—and a national church was a contradiction in terms. Such imposition was (and this metaphor Williams would repeat) 'spiritual rape.'

He concluded the *Queries* with a rapid-fire series of assertions: this 'Moses' shadow' of an Assembly was contrary to the New Testament model; to the true nature of civil magistracy; to the hope of Jews being converted (and so to bringing in the millennium) as it would prevent them living in the land; it was opposed to civil peace, as imposed religion either produces hypocritical conformists among the pliable, or makes persecuted victims of the conscientious objector. After 1,600 years of bloodshed, it was time to forsake Moses and follow Christ.

Parliament, dominated by Presbyterians, was in no mood to listen. In order to secure Scottish support for the war effort, it had, in September 1643, agreed the Solemn League and Covenant with the Scots, accepting the imposition of Presbyterianism as the price of support against the king although Sir Henry Vane had inserted a reservation that the reformation of worship should be founded directly on the Word of God rather than on the practice of the Scots. In February 1644 all men over eighteen had to swear allegiance to the Solemn League and Covenant. Enforcement was not strict, but it was a movement away from toleration. In spring 1644 legislation enforced strict observance of the Sabbath, no games or sports, no trade or travel, the removal of maypoles. Preaching, like printing, had to be licensed. Sectarianism was erupting everywhere, not least in Cromwell's army. It had to be checked. Individual congregations would not be allowed to 'take up what worship they pleased.' Rhode Island had its charter, but old England was not at this moment leaning towards tolerance.

Williams was not finished yet. On 15 July, before leaving London, he had his largest and greatest work published.

Chapter 9

The Bloudy Tenent

THE BLOUDY TENENT (WE MIGHT CALL IT THE BLOODTHIRSTY 'PRINCIPLE,' or 'Tenet') of Persecution for Cause of Conscience, discussed ...' was written, Williams tells us, 'in changes of rooms or corners' in London, even when out in the country gathering wood, in fields and strange houses, when travelling,' when he had been 'forced to gather and scatter his loose thoughts and papers.' The first part of the book argues for liberty of conscience. It begins with the reproduction of the letter of a prisoner in Newgate, believed to be the Baptist John Murton, who addressed King James in 1616 pleading for liberty of conscience. Apparently the letter was written in milk brought to Murton in prison, on paper smuggled in as the bottle top, the writing becoming visible when heated. That is followed by an answer to Murton written in about 1634 by John Cotton, after Murton's letter had been sent to him for comment. Williams' reply to Cotton is the substance of the first half of *The Bloudy Tenent*. The second part of the book (though there is much overlapping between the two sections) argues for the separation of church and state and takes the form of a response to *A Model of Church and Civil Power* produced by New England ministers to explain and justify the New England form of government in 1635, particularly the right of magistrates to block the appointment by Salem of Williams as their teacher.

Arguments for liberty of conscience had been made before; calls for liberty of conscience for *everyone* were virtually unknown; neither Milton nor, later, John Locke would have permitted liberty for Roman Catholics, nor would Locke for atheists. Calls for separation of church and state were rare indeed. Thomas Helwys had argued for it; other Separatists had called for toleration but had not challenged the basic principle of state power over the church. Most Puritans would have agreed that conscience is subject to reason and can only be persuaded by the power of divine truth, but they would also have held that the obligation to co-operate with establishing the godly commonwealth took precedence over the liberty to believe what one liked. Roger Williams cut the Gordian knot by challenging the whole vision of a godly commonwealth.

The form the book takes is a dialogue between Truth and Peace. 'Truth and Peace' was a catchphrase of the Parliamentarians; they struck a coin with the words on. In Williams' book Truth and Peace lament the absence of both liberty of conscience and the separation of church and state; Truth and Peace would both benefit from the enjoyment of those principles. Like Milton on the freedom of the press, Williams sees nothing to fear, so far as Christianity is concerned, from intellectual and religious freedom, indeed much to be gained.

Williams writes a preface to the Houses of Parliament. He tells the members that next to saving their own souls their great task as *Christians* is to save the souls of others, 'but as *magistrates* [i.e. rulers] the bodies and goods, of others' (my italics). He promised arguments from religion, reason and experience to prove that the state should not impose religion. The bulk of his book is directly or indirectly the interpretation of Scripture. He profoundly hoped that no future generation, nor Rome nor Oxford (respectively at that time the homes of the papacy and the Church of England in the person of the king) should ever be told that 'the parliament of England hath committed a greater rape [i.e. coercing consciences] than if they had forced or ravished the bodies of all the women in the world.' He quotes Sir Francis Bacon: 'Such as hold pressure of conscience, are guided therein by some private interests of their own.'[1] On the second page of the book proper he refers to Sir Edward Coke. The big guns were being wheeled into position.

A second preface is 'to every courteous reader':

> In vain have English parliaments permitted English bibles in the poorest English houses, and the simplest man or woman to search the scriptures, if yet against their souls persuasion from the scripture they should be forced, as if they lived in Spain or Rome itself without the sight of a bible, to believe as the church believes ... Having bought truth dear, we must not sell it cheap, not the least grain of it for the whole world; no not for the saving of souls, though our own most precious.

In a foreword he summarizes his case in twelve propositions, the fundamental one being:

> It is the will and command of God that, since the coming of his Son the Lord Jesus, a permission of the most Paganish, Jewish, Turkish, or anti-christian consciences and worships be granted to all men in all nations and countries: and they are only to be fought against with that sword which is only, in soul matters, able to conquer: to wit, the sword of God's Spirit, the word of God.

By 'permission' it should be noted, Williams does not mean that God approves of all beliefs—merely that they are allowed to exist for the time being. Correlative to this are the propositions (amongst others) that: all civil states are essentially civil and are no judges in spiritual matters; the state of Israel is figurative and ceremonial and no pattern or precedent for any kingdom in the world to follow; God does not require a uniformity of religion in any civil state, and any such enforced uniformity is the greatest occasion of civil war, ravishing of conscience, persecution of Christians and of hypocrisy and destruction of millions of souls; enforcing uniformity necessarily disclaims our desires and hopes of the Jews' conversion to Christ; liberty of conscience alone can procure a lasting peace in a nation; and true civility and Christianity may flourish in a state, 'notwithstanding the permission of diverse and contrary consciences.'

Conscience

Taking up the arguments of John Murton and more particularly John Cotton's answer to Murton, the first section of the book is Williams' plea for liberty of conscience. No-one argued against the right of the church to discipline members or prosecute heresy. The issue was whether the state had any right to do so. In replying to Murton, Cotton said that no-one should be persecuted for conscience 'rightly informed' and if their conscience was 'wrongly informed' or 'misinformed' they should not be punished unless, either his error was fundamental *or* it was seditiously and turbulently promoted, *and* that after due conviction of his conscience ('being admonished once or twice'—Titus 3:10) he still persists in his wrong doctrine or practice.[2] Building on Titus 3:10 (which is about church discipline, whereas Cotton is seeking to argue for the state's administering of punishment for wrong belief or practice) Cotton said that the reason one can punish is:

> Because in fundamental and principal points of doctrine or worship, the word of God in such things is so clear, that he cannot but be convinced in conscience of the dangerous error of his way after once or twice admonition, wisely and faithfully dispensed.

In other words, if you believe differently from what is considered the 'clear' Word of God, on an important issue, and you stick to that after you have been 'wisely and faithfully' admonished once or twice, you can be punished by the state for heresy or malpractice. If anyone persists, said Cotton, it is not out of conscience but 'against his conscience.' So if after due admonition you persist in the wrong belief or act, you can be punished and are 'not persecuted for cause of conscience but for sinning against conscience.' Christians so sinning against the light of faith and conscience can be censured by the church with excommunication and by the 'civil sword' also, in case 'they shall corrupt others to the perdition of their souls.' 'Heretics,' after due admonition, should not be tolerated either in the church or the state to 'preserve others from dangerous and damnable infection.'

The logic of Cotton's position of course is that only an orthodox (Puritan) believer could be adjudged to have a good conscience. A 'heretic' *ipso facto* has a guilty conscience and cannot be adjudged to be acting with sincerity. Moreover he can legitimately be banished from the state, not just excommunicated from a church. In the end the Puritans were prepared to grant freedom of conscience only 'to men that fear God.'

Setting the scene biblically, Truth reminds Peace that these heavens and earth are passing away, and we look for a new heavens and earth wherein dwells righteousness (2 Peter 3:13). Meanwhile we must 'bear the fury of the dragon's wrath.' How few 'witnesses in sackcloth' (Revelation 11:3) there are to plead for the truth!

Williams weighs in with some general arguments against Cotton's position. Such arguments rely more on Moses (and the Old Testament) than on Christ, he notes; many believers have erred on fundamentals regarding the church. What about ministers who remained in the Church of England? Did they not have enough light to leave? And what of Cotton in England worshipping according to the Prayer Book? Was not that a fundamental matter in which he could be said to have 'sinned against conscience?' He turned against the Prayer Book quickly enough when he came to New England.

What then is 'persecution for cause of conscience?' Not physical mistreatment alone; rather 'to molest any person, Jew or Gentile, for either professing doctrine, or practising worship merely religious or spiritual, it is to persecute him;' and further, that if anyone 'dares not be constrained to yield obedience to such doctrines and worships as are by men invented and appointed,'[3] such as the young Jews in the fiery furnace—that is, either to hinder someone from doing what they believe to be right, or to force them to do what they believe to be wrong (and here Williams would say that one should not be forced even to believe or do the truth).

Our state's walls are the churches, said the Puritans; but the walls of the church are made up of living stones, not of people forced to worship, responded Williams.[4]

Williams then deals with some of the Scriptures first raised by Murton and answered by Cotton. A key passage is the parable of the wheat and tares (Matthew 13:24–43). Cotton's argument was that by 'world' Jesus means 'by a usual trope [figure of speech], the church scattered throughout the world.' The tares said Cotton are partial hypocrites, very similar to wheat, or, 'partly such doctrines or practices that are indeed unsound,' but yet come so near the truth that good men may be taken with them; to remove them would be to risk taking the wheat too so the Lord Jesus calls for toleration. (In a later reply to Williams, Cotton withdrew the claim that the tares could be doctrines or practices—they were people). In other words, you do not discipline hypocrites who resemble true believers. No, wrong, said Williams, tares are antichristian idolaters, obvious unbelievers, not hypocrites. Do you not discipline a known hypocrite in a church? The field, as Jesus said, is not the church but the world. Toleration as taught by Jesus here is of such persons in the world, not of hypocrites in the church—and that in the end will be for the good of the church.[5] Cotton is mingling church and state; the parable has nothing to do with church government.

Isaiah 49:23 (KJV) was a favourite text of those who favoured civil magistracy superintending the church—'And kings shall be thy nursing fathers, and their queens thy nursing mothers: they shall bow down to thee with their face toward the earth, and lick up the dust of thy feet; and thou shalt know that I am the LORD.' Williams was not unhappy to use the verse so long as their nursing was limited to the body and goods of citizens. After all what did it mean that the supposed 'supreme governor' of the church should lick the dust of the church's feet?

Williams argued (we might think a bit optimistically) that 'Dead man cannot be infected,' and God's sheep are safe in his hands, so what harm can heresy do to the world?[6] In the church of course it must be disciplined. A false religion outside the church cannot hurt the church; and will not hurt the civil state provided no civil law is broken.[7] It is worth noting that 'heresy' in New England at this time included denying: the baptizing of infants, the ordinance of magistracy and their authority to make war or punish offenders against the first table; such a heretic was to be banished from the jurisdiction.

A favourite theme was that people of other religions or none could be good citizens. He was not just thinking of Christianized Europeans; he had in mind the Native Americans he knew so well—and about whom he was not romantic.

The adequacy of the spiritual weapons provided by the Lord

was also repeatedly argued by Williams. Were Cotton and others saying that the Lord had not sufficiently provided for the church? Did the church have to rely on the arm of the state, on the sword of steel as well as the sword of the Spirit?[8] Was Christ to be made a temporal king by force asked Williams? It was a direct advancing of Christ's purpose of saving souls 'to destroy (if need be) the bodies of those wolves who seek to destroy the souls of those for whom Christ died,' replied Cotton.[9] No, 'soul killers' are to be dealt with by spiritual weapons, insisted Williams. Just think—they may be converted! Was not Paul once Saul?

What then of Romans 13—the classic biblical passage on Christian obligation to the authorities? Williams points out that this is in the context, after Romans 12, of a Christian's duties in the church, then in the world, and then to the state, and generally our duty of love to all (Romans 13:9–14). The emperors to whom Paul counsels obedience were certainly not converted, he reminds us; and will we say Christ has committed the care of his church to them? Did not Paul appeal to the emperor (Acts 25:11)? Yes, replied Williams but only in civil matters, not spiritual. But, Cotton asked, is not the magistrate to punish evil (Romans 13:4) and is not spiritual error and deception the worst sort of evil; and if religion is the best good for a state, should not the magistrate assist the church in promoting it?[10] The emperor is only to deal with evil and good in relation to bodies and goods, says Williams, not spiritual good or evil which he is incompetent to judge. Yet Williams does agree that rulers should punish immorality—such as when the Roman emperor punished Ovid for 'teaching the wanton art of love, leading to and ushering on lasciviousness and uncleanness.'[11]

A section on testimonies of famous princes follows, as cited by John Murton and discussed by Cotton, including Stephen of Poland, the king of Bohemia and James I. Williams moves on. He sees the problem of Christendom beginning with Constantine. Constantine was more a threat to the church than Nero, said Williams; the garden of the church was turned into the wilderness of the whole nation. Before Constantine the church was fragrant in persecution. To this mixing of church and state could be traced the New England law of 1631, whereby only church members could be 'freemen' and every inhabitant was compelled to support the church. '[A] national church, which elsewhere [Cotton] professes against, a state-church, whether explicit, as in old England, or implicit, as in New, is not the institution of the Lord Jesus Christ.'[12]

Persecution for conscience' sake is nothing less than 'soul rape.' Moreover liberty of conscience should be enjoyed by all, not just by those who fear God; to demand otherwise is to create either hypocrites or persecution, and to make the state the judge of souls. It was indeed hypocritical of the Puritans, Williams could not resist pointing out, to be loud in protesting against persecution when they were 'under hatches' but becoming persecutors once they were 'at the helm.'[13]

To summarize, Williams' main arguments for the inviolability of the conscience were:

(i) God alone is Lord of the conscience; no 'civil magistrate, no king, nor Caesar, have any power over the souls or consciences of their subjects, in the matters of God and the crown of Jesus.'

(ii) Coercion does not work anyway as conscience is subject only to the rules of understanding which effect change by reason, argument and persuasion. The Bible after all only gives us the Word of the Spirit as our sword.

(iii) Coercion creates hypocrites.

(iv) Coercion confirms people in their erroneous convictions.

(v) Coercion will eventually turn against the true church.

(vi) Coercion hardens people's hearts and causes them to transgress their moral faculties, severing moral co-operation between the will and the intellect, in short to choose irrationally and without conviction.

(vii) 'That religion cannot be true which needs such instruments of violence to uphold it.' At times for the public good a person may have to be coerced against conscience (say a man conscientiously believed in polygamy) but this was still a violation albeit a justified one.

Church and state

A Model of Church and Civil Power did not have legal force but it embodied so much of what became ecclesiastical or civil law, and so clearly expressed the church-state relationship in New England, that Williams did well to use it as a statement of views he opposed. Its expressed premise was that while God has given distinct powers to church (the keys) and commonwealth (the sword), every soul in the church is subject to the state and every member of the commonwealth is a member of the church. The issue for the *Model* to elucidate was how the respective powers may be exercised without infringing on each other. A favourite Scripture of the Puritans in this regard, as mentioned earlier, was Isaiah 49:23. Williams was more inclined to begin with Jesus' words in Mark 12:17 (KJV), 'Render to Caesar the things that are Caesar's, and to God the things that are God's;' or John 18:36, 'My kingdom is not of this world.' The two kingdoms were not inconsistent but separate.

According to the *Model* the purpose of the state is to procure and preserve external and temporal peace (1 Timothy 2:1–2); the purpose of the church, to create internal and spiritual peace. Magistrates have power in religion to see that outward peace is preserved so have power over both tables of the law to preserve godliness. No, said Williams; 1 Timothy 2:1–2 simply exhorts us to pray for the government. The government has authority in religion only to protect freedom of worship for all, not to determine what that religion should be or to impose a particular religion or forms of worship. It is impossible that Christ would appoint such ignorant and idolatrous men as most rulers are, to guard his bride.[14] According to the *Model* civil peace cannot survive where religion is corrupted; the state must ensure church officers do their duty.

Basic to Williams' thought was that 'a civil government is an ordinance of God, to conserve the civil peace of people so far as concerns their bodies and goods,' but, more radically, he continues, 'from this grant I infer ... that the sovereign, original, and foundation of civil power, lies in the people.'[15] His view was that magistracy (government) in general came from God, but its particular forms came from the people. 'Gentile princes ... whether monarchical, aristocratical, or democratical; who, though government in general be from God, yet, receive their callings, power and authority, both kings and parliaments, mediately from the people,' he wrote.[16]

Similar views were not unusual at the time. Samuel Rutherford in *Lex, Rex*, in defending the rights of the people against tyranny, argues that while the office of kingship is from God, and God sovereignly guides the people, yet, 'The power of creating a [particular] man a king is from the people.'[17] He illustrates this from the Old Testament: God 'extraordinarily designed' men to be kings 'yet were they never actually installed kings till the people made them kings.' Rutherford carefully balances divine sovereignty and human activity. God institutes a ruler but through the mediation of the people. As William Symington puts it, 'government is at once the ordinance of God and an ordinance of man.' Man settles his own constitution and chooses the particular ruler; but the institution of government itself is of God.[18]

Rutherford avoids the 'natural rights' notion of government being the creation of man; but on the other hand he steers clear of denying the people any part in appointing their king. Rutherford also allows that God uses the 'aptitude and temper' of each commonwealth 'to determine the wills and liberty of people to pitch upon' the right form of government for them, just as he guides people into single or married life. His favoured form of government however was aristocracy, growing out of fatherly government.

It is not so clear that Williams keeps the balance as well as Rutherford, and leans in the direction of 'natural rights.' John Locke certainly developed that view. Williams firmly, however, believed government to be an ordinance of God.

Note that Williams is not thinking as a liberal political theorist so much as a seventeenth century theologian here; the principal point he makes from the assertion that the foundation of civil power lies in the people, is that it is quite wrong, therefore, to allow the civil government power over the church. If people make the government and the magistrate has the power over the church (as New England and virtually every other government at that time asserted), then the people (that is, all people, of any religious persuasion or none) were effectively governing the church. Surely this is 'to pull God, and Christ, and Spirit out of heaven.'[19] What, says Williams, if churches were set up among the Natives? Would their governments have authority over those churches? His objection was not to a Native American government as such; only to the idea that any government, be it Puritan or

Native, had authority over the church. The tacit assumption of the Puritans was always that the governors would be Christian—their kind of Christian.

As to the form of government, Williams continues, 'the people may erect and establish what form of government seems to them most meet for their civil condition.'[20] In Rhode Island, of course, that would be a democracy with 'liberty and equality' in all things. Theoretically it sounds as if Williams would countenance other forms of government, but his principles were unswervingly in the direction of democracy.

The walls of our state are made of 'the stones of the churches,' wrote the New England ministers. Williams responded that where states only approve the worship they like, soon Christ and his bride are driven out. He always envisaged that force in religious matters would be turned against the true church in the end. 'And when,' he asked more than once, following Murton, 'did you see Christ, his apostles and the early church relying on the arm of government to spread the word of the Kingdom and build the church?' Look at the changes in the history of England in the century and a half before Williams wrote. As for James and Charles—as a young man Williams had met them both and knew how unsuited they were to be the 'supreme governor' of any church. This is what happens when *Cuius regio, eius religio* ('Whose the Realm, His the religion') is the ruling principle.

The lynchpin of Williams' case against 'the New England way' as represented by Cotton and the *Model* was that Israel was a 'type' and the church is the 'antitype.' True Israelites are the spiritual children of Abraham (Galatians 3:16). Williams traces the biblical narrative of the land of Canaan, the people, kingship and priesthood, the laws, wars and enemies of Israel to prove his point. He scorned popular metaphors like 'Hippocrates' twins' for a close relation between church and state. The Ten

Commandments he saw as being of universal application, ('the second table contains the law of nature') but to Israel he gave them twice on Sinai and yet again to spiritual Israel 'the people and the church of God, in whose hearts of flesh he writes his laws (Jer. 31).' The putting to death of a false prophet is a type of church discipline; material prosperity the type of spiritual prosperity. 'The want of discerning this true parallel between Israel in the type then, and Israel the antitype now, is that rock whereon, through the Lord's righteous jealousy, punishing the world and chastising his people, thousands dash, and make woeful shipwreck.'[21]

Israel and her institutions may be imitated but they are not authoritative for the modern state. The apostles recognized the legitimacy of other nations and their laws.

Williams also outlined his belief that in the church there were two types of ministry, one for converting, such as the apostles had, and the second for feeding and nourishing the flock as pastors and teachers. To neither ministry did Jesus or the apostles compel people (and he deals with the injunction in the parable 'compel them to come in' (Luke 14:23) to exclude physical force and legal compulsion). Williams' singular views about there being no validly authorized converting ministry today—the Great Commission (Matthew 28:16–20), he believed, only applying to the apostles—meant that there could be no valid churches today unless God, perhaps, 'extraordinarily stirred up' someone with new apostolic authority.[22] Certainly no magistrate had the power to 'send' a minister.

As for magistrates, it was too much for them to be expected to rule the church. Had God endowed them with gifts to govern the church? Did they not have more than enough to do governing the state? Did Jesus or the apostles try to do both?

What does the ruler owe the church? If he believes a religion to be true, he owes it his personal allegiance as a man; and protection of its adherents. If he believes it to be false, he owes it permission to exist 'for public peace and quiet's sake' and protection of its adherents, as his subjects, as to their persons and goods.[23] No magistrate may bring in set forms of prayer, nor ceremonies, nor govern acts of worship. The civil magistrate trying to govern the church was like a passenger, however high-born, trying to tell the master or pilot of a ship how to steer his vessel.

Was there no difference if a man were a Christian? Yes, said Williams:

A Christian captain, Christian merchant, physician, lawyer, pilot, father, master, and so consequently magistrate etc., is no more a captain, merchant, physician, lawyer, pilot, father, master, magistrate etc. than a captain, merchant etc. of any other conscience or religion. It is true, Christianity teaches all these to act in their several callings to a higher ultimate end, from higher principles, in a more heavenly and spiritual manner, etc. .... [The believer] acts from a root of the fear of God and love to mankind in his whole course ... His aim is more to glorify God than to gain his pay, or make his voyage ... he walks heavenly with men and God, in a constant observation of God's hand in storms, calms etc. So that the thread of navigation being equally spun by a believing and unbelieving pilot, yet is it drawn over with the gold of godliness and Christianity by a Christian pilot, while he is holy in all manner of Christianity (1 Pet. 1:15). But lastly, the Christian pilot's power over the souls and consciences of his sailors and passengers is not greater than that of the anti-christian, otherwise than he can subdue the souls of any by the two-edged sword of the Spirit, the word of God, and by his holy demeanour in his place, etc.[24]

Economically too it was far from proven (for prosperity was looked on as a sign of God's approval) that God blessed those nations where the state enforced godliness, or tried to. 'Event and success come alike to all.'[25] Indeed the evidence of recent history suggested that God favoured Catholics over Protestants. You could also turn the 'toleration leads to God's curse' argument on its head. Look at Holland. Amsterdam, once a small fishing town, was a haven for 'dissenting consciences' and now a world power. New England's principle of 'civil rights for church members only' shut out some of the best servants of the state for civil office. Pagan governments, like that of Cyrus (Ezra 1:1–4) or Artaxerxes (Ezra 7:23) can treat a religion fairly without in any sense sharing the same aims as, or establishing, that religion.

Further no-one could seriously argue that the church is essential to civil peace—even 'the very Americans and wildest pagans keep the peace of their towns or cities, though neither in one nor the other can any man prove a true church of God in those places and consequently no spiritual or heavenly peace.'[26] An illustration Williams uses to describe the place of the church in relation to the state is that of an association within a city:

> The Church or company of worshippers, whether true or false, is like unto a body or college of physicians in a city—like unto a corporation, society or company of East India or Turkey merchants, or any other society or company in London: which companies may hold their courts, keep their records, hold disputations, and in matters concerning their society may dissent, divide, break into schisms and factions, sue and implead each other at the law, yea, wholly break up and dissolve into pieces and nothing, and yet the peace of the city not be in the least measure impaired or disturbed; because the essence or being of the city and so the well-being and peace thereof is essentially distinct from those particular societies ... For instance further, the city or civil state of Ephesus was essentially distinct from the worship of Diana in the city ... Again, the church of Christ in Ephesus ... was distinct from both.[27]

To summarize his views on separation of church and state:

(i) God has, since the coming of Christ, permitted complete freedom of conscience and worship be granted to all men in all nations and countries and idolatry and unbelief are only to be fought against with the sword of the Spirit, the Word of God.

(ii) Although government is an ordinance of God, all civil states are essentially civil and are not competent in spiritual matters; the state's authority derives from people; the church must not be placed under the 'world.'

(iii) It will lead to the church becoming a wilderness.

(iv) The state of Israel is figurative and no authoritative pattern or precedent for any kingdom in the world to follow.

(v) Spiritual gifts, offices and weapons are sufficient to deal with spiritual enemies and problems; the church does not need the state either to establish or preserve churches.

(vi) State coercion in religion is the greatest occasion of civil war, violating of conscience, persecution of Christians and of hypocrisy and destruction of millions of souls.

(vii) State-church separation alone can procure a lasting peace in a nation.

(viii) True civility and Christianity may flourish in a state, 'notwithstanding the permission of diverse and contrary consciences' e.g. Holland.

(ix) Civil duties of obedience and participation remain.

Back home

'Somehow the message survives the medium,' is Edwin Gaustad's wry comment on Williams' untidy but powerful book.[28] It also survived a hostile reception. William Prynne, who had suffered for writing against the immorality of stage plays in 1634, now showed that the persecuted are not necessarily tolerant. He condemned Williams' 'dangerous Licentious Book' for suggesting that a person be 'left free to his own free liberty of conscience.' Published in July 1644, it was ordered by Parliament to be burned in August and the Licenser was rebuked for letting it through. By then Williams was on board ship back to New England. He had his charter in his bag; he also had a letter from prominent names in Parliament commending him and putting pressure (successfully) on Massachusetts to grant him safe passage through their colony on his way back to Providence. When he returned to Rhode Island his welcome was warmer. Fourteen canoes crowded about the Seekonk River to give their hero a suitable greeting. Mary and he were reunited, with their sixth and last child, Joseph, born in December 1643. The colony appointed him their chief officer, a position he held for three years. It was a rewarding time. But there was much work to be done.

Chapter 10

Trying To Make It Work

Correspondence with John Cotton

THERE WAS ANOTHER STRAND OF CORRESPONDENCE WITH JOHN COTTON in addition to the letter answered in *The Bloudy Tenent*. A letter Cotton wrote to Williams shortly after his banishment in 1636 was published in London in 1643 and in 1644 Williams published a reply in *Mr Cottons Letter Lately Printed, Examined and Answered*.[1] The letter was a justification of the banishment from the point of view of Massachusetts and Cotton personally. In it we have the four reasons outlined in Chapter 4 for his banishment. We also get some insight into Williams' thinking about his own ministry. He was a 'poor despised ram's horn'—a witness in sackcloth. He denies that he 'banished himself,' as Cotton alleges; and if church and state are separate, why does Cotton call the banishment from the state, which it was, a banishment from 'the churches?'

The undeniable fact is that Massachusetts operated an implicitly national church. They claimed to have turned their back on the corruptions of the Church of England, yet not left the Church itself; they were establishing a congregational system but it was in practice a national church. Cotton said that God afflicted Williams in autumn 1635 because, 'it pleased him to stop your mouth by a sudden illness.' Cotton, alleges Williams, says that being regenerate was not enough to be a church member; Williams agreed that a Christian should also separate himself from a corrupt church. But then, the Congregationalists in New England tested regeneration more rigorously than those in old England. Williams accused Cotton of walking between Christ and anti-Christ. Cotton called it walking between two extremes. Williams responded—this 'middle walking' is 'halting' (that is, limping) between two opinions. Puritans suffered more for their principles than Separatists, said Cotton; not at all said Williams, citing the executions of Penry, Barrowe and Greenwood under Elizabeth. Anyway, all Separatists began as Puritans. Referring with approval to John Canne, he wrote:

> The principles of the puritans against bishops and ceremonies, and profaneness of people professing Christ, and the necessity of Christ's flock and discipline, must necessarily, if truly followed, lead on to and enforce a separation from such ways, worships and worshippers, to seek out the true way of God's worship according to Christ Jesus.[2]

Towards the close of his reply to Cotton, Williams used a metaphor that resonates today:

> First, the faithful labours of many witnesses of Jesus Christ, extant to the world, abundantly proving, that the church of the Jews under the Old Testament in the type, and the church of the Christians under the New Testament in the antitype, were both separate from the world; and that when they have opened a gap in the hedge, or wall of separation, between the garden of the church and the wilderness of the world, God hath ever broke down the wall itself,

removed the candlestick, etc., and made his garden a wilderness, as at this day. And that therefore if he will ever please to restore his garden and paradise again, it must of necessity be walled in peculiarly unto himself from the world, and that all that shall be saved out of the world are to be transplanted out of the wilderness of the world, and added unto his church or garden.[3]

The phrase 'wall of separation' has become famous, or infamous, as used by Thomas Jefferson in a letter in 1802 to Baptists in Danbury, Connecticut. His reference however was to a wall between the church and the state—a political distinction. Williams is referring to the spiritual distinction between the church and the world. Williams is also concerned to save the church from corruption, not (here at least) to avoid church domination of the state. There is no evidence of dependence by Jefferson on Williams though that does not mean there was none. At the time of the American War of Independence, Baptist scholars such as Isaac Backus were making Williams' thought known. Today the phrase has become a tool in Supreme Court interpretation of the First Amendment to the United States Constitution which provides that 'Congress shall make no law respecting an establishment of religion, or prohibiting the free exercise thereof.' It is used to prise ever wider the gap between religion and public life and to restrict religious exercise to the private sphere. Williams would probably (one can never be sure) have been happy with the First Amendment; he would probably have agreed too, *contra* many on the American religious right that public confessions of religion, prayers in schools and on civic occasions should be avoided; they are an imposition (he would say) on the consciences of unbelievers and create hypocrisy, resentment or indifference, depending on the sensitivity of the person concerned.

Cotton replied to Williams in 1647, defending the actions of

Massachusetts and his own part in Williams' expulsion. He wrote, 'banishment in this country is not counted so much a confinement as an enlargement, where a man does not so much lose civil comforts, as change them.'[4] Williams would hardly have been impressed with that thought.

As for *The Bloudy Tenent*, between 1644 and 1649 over sixty pamphlets directly addressed Williams and at least 120 more quoted him, according to John Barry. Robert Baillie, the Scottish Commissioner at the Westminster Assembly, who had called Williams his 'good acquaintance' and spoke well of his personal qualities, alleged that the concept that sovereignty lay in the people was the 'master of our disorders.' The radical Levellers, led by John Lilburne, pursuing democracy, quoted Williams verbatim in their literature. Some called for toleration in Parliament, but, says Barry:

> Most of those seeking toleration still wanted only Protestant dissent allowed—they wanted to prohibit Catholic worship and often Anglican worship as well. Virtually all but Williams still condemned atheism as a serious crime. And Williams still remained largely isolated in calling for the utter separation of church and state—the complete disengagement of one from the other.[5]

So what went on in Rhode Island after Williams' triumphant return in 1644?

Struggles in state-making

As Robert Baillie and Sir Henry Vane debated toleration in England, Williams was arriving in Massachusetts. He passed through to his welcome in Providence. The different visions of the two states would become increasingly apparent. For Winthrop and Cotton it was 'to sanctify a nation,' to produce a godly commonwealth, the state helping the church towards the same end. A Mosaic legal code so far as possible would be enforced.

The pursuit of purity, of doing God's will, could easily degenerate in such a context into the pressure to conform or make others conform. Williams did not conform and had no desire to make others do so.

Yet he too sought God's will. Williams was always saved from sliding towards the mysticism and Gnostic individualism of the Hutchinsonians, Samuel Gorton, Fifth Monarchists, Seekers and the Quakers by his devotion to Scripture as essential to knowing God, and to the external ordinances of the church (one day to be purely restored). Believing that the 'apostolic succession' initiated by Christ had been lost in the apostasy of the Middle Ages, that the restoration of the true, primitive church awaited Christ's appointment of a new order of apostles, he was meanwhile a 'prophet in sackcloth,' waiting with groups of like-minded Christians for that day. To find the truth, it was essential that freedom of conscience be permitted, that the state therefore exercise no authority in the church. He was on his own in the clarity and persistence with which he insisted on *universal* freedom of conscience and the *absolute* separation of church and state; on his own too in the consistency with which he lived out his beliefs. Williams was no ivory tower theologian. He lived what he believed.

He lived it too for others, and some of his toughest tests would arise after his return from London with the charter. William Coddington, the founder of Newport on Aquidneck Island, tried to prevent any colony-wide government and proposed to Winthrop that Newport and Portsmouth be incorporated into Plymouth or Massachusetts. Winthrop's hitherto friendly demeanour to Williams had changed. The Massachusetts magistrates now claimed all of Rhode Island under the invalid charter obtained by Thomas Weld in London.

Nonetheless Williams as chief officer until 1647 managed to hold

Boston at bay, and Rhode Island began to settle down. He sought to extend property rights on a basis of 'liberty and equality.' In Massachusetts, Cotton called for 'men of eminent quality and descent' to be given large holdings; the Grand Court granted thirty-two such men a total of 57,214 acres and large grants were also given by the towns. One Massachusetts town was persuaded by its minister to allow only those 'as might be fit for Church members' to acquire land. In Rhode Island, Williams fought for young single men, newcomers, to be given land holdings on payment of ten shillings. In 1646 the Committee on Foreign Plantations in London led by the Earl of Warwick, declared the settlement of Shawomet to belong to Rhode Island. Samuel Gorton, who had been fighting for this in England, returned to Rhode Island, claimed his property and renamed it Warwick after the Earl.

In May 1647 representatives of Providence, Newport, Portsmouth and Warwick met to frame the constitution that in John Barry's words 'created the freest society in the world.'[6] The government was reaffirmed as 'Democratical: that is to say, a Government held by the free and voluntary consent of all, or the greater part of the free inhabitants.' Freedom of religion was confirmed and 'a solemn profession' would have 'as full force as an oath.' Williams produced a 'Modell' of laws for the colony which evinced greater respect for social equality before the law than other Puritan charters. Outlawed, among other crimes, were murder, misbehaviour, robbery, wanton destruction of property, 'batteries and assaults,' adultery, fornication, rape, whore-mongering, fraudulent dealing, forgery, 'liars,' perjury, breach of covenant, slander, drunkenness, 'loafing at alehouses' and swearing and cursing. One day in seven was fixed for rest and recreation for servants and residents. Penalties tended to be milder. In Williams' lifetime, only two men were executed, both for murder. A weakness of the constitution was its inadequate provision for schools; education suffered at first because it was only left to local initiatives.

Williams became assistant governor after being chief officer. He spent much of his time at his trading post twenty miles south of Providence at Cocumscussoc, present-day Wickford, laid out for him by Canonicus' 'own hand.' His trading was making him £100 a year; he owned several small canoes, a 'great Canow,' a pinnace and a shallop. He relished his 'beloved privacie.' He also wrote, responding with *The Bloudy Tenent Yet More Bloudy* to Cotton's 1647 work *The Bloudy Tenent, Washed ....* Other works too came from his restless and fertile mind, as we shall see, though nothing would be published until a forthcoming visit to London.

Sadly this became necessary. William Coddington tried to persuade Massachusetts to seize Rhode Island. He went to London and in 1651 after two years' manoeuvring he obtained a charter for a new plantation of Aquidneck Island and the towns of Newport and Portsmouth. The charter made him governor for life. The inhabitants of the towns, however, refused to accept him and he fled to Boston. But Williams now had to go to England again to protect the colony's interests. He sailed in November 1651. With him he took John Clarke, founder and minister of the second Baptist church in America in Newport, the colony's attorney general, William Dyer, and his wife Mary.

Baptists punished in Boston

Four months before he sailed Williams sent the manuscript of *The Bloudy Tenent Yet More Bloudy* for publication. Meanwhile in July 1651 John Clarke with fellow Baptists Obadiah Holmes and John Crandall visited an elderly blind Baptist, William Witter, in Lynn, Massachusetts. Clarke preached a sermon in his house. They were arrested. A law in Massachusetts passed in 1644 banished anyone who opposed infant baptism or denied that a magistrate had the right to punish breaches of the first table of the Decalogue. In 1645 Massachusetts had passed a law banning Baptists from the colony. Holmes had already been excommunicated and banned from the colony for baptizing people by immersion. Because of his prior ban, Holmes was fined £30, Clarke £20 and Crandall £5. Someone paid Clarke's fine for him without his knowledge and he was released. For conscience' sake Holmes refused to allow anyone to pay his fine and in consequence he received thirty lashes with a three-cord whip so that one man who saw him later wondered how he could live after it. For several days he was only able to sleep by kneeling on his hands and knees.

Governor Endecott said that they 'deserved death, and he would not have such trash brought into his jurisdiction.' John Cotton preached a sermon before the court in which he said that 'denying infant baptism would overthrow all; and it was a capital offence and therefore they were foul murderers.'[7]

Sir Richard Saltonstall, a founder member of the Massachusetts Bay Company, soon wrote to Rev. John Wilson and John Cotton, grieving to hear, 'what sad things are reported daily of your tyranny and persecutions in New England, as that you fine, whip and imprison men for their consciences.' Sounding very like Williams he chided them for compelling in matters of worship, for to compel men:

> To do that whereof they are not persuaded is to make them sin, for so the apostle tells us, and many are made hypocrites thereby, conforming in their outward man for fear of punishment ... These rigid ways have laid you very low in the hearts of the saints.'[8]

Cotton responded that it was

> better to be hypocrites than profane persons. Hypocrites give God part of His due, the outward man, but the profane person gives God neither outward nor inward man.[9]

The following year, 1652, Clarke wrote '*Ill Newes from New England: or A Narrative of New Englands Persecution* which increased concern in Parliament and in the mind of Oliver Cromwell about Massachusetts' intolerance. Williams wrote to John Endecott pleading for liberty of conscience and an end to persecution, but his plea went unheeded. He appended a copy of the letter to *The Bloudy Tenent Yet More Bloudy* as a 'Testimony to Mr Clark's Narrative.'

Before leaving for England, Williams sold his trading post and other assets to finance his trip. He also wrote to Massachusetts for permission to sail from Boston. It was granted. Williams, Clarke and Dyer arrived in England. It was three years after the king had been executed and England was in a state of social turmoil and political paralysis. Peter Ackroyd describes it this way:

> The condition of England was enough to cause dismay. The late wars had badly injured trade, with a consequent steep increase in unemployment; bands of beggars roamed the land in numbers not seen since the last century. The country gentry and other landowners were devastated by the various taxes imposed upon them; those who favoured the royalist cause found their lands in danger of confiscation or sale. The prisons were filled with debtors. The Church was in confusion, with radical sectaries and orthodox believers still engaged in recrimination and complaint. Episcopacy had been abolished but no other form of national church government had taken its place; it was said that the mass of people could not find ministers to serve them. Many called, without success, for legislation to abolish burdensome taxes, to simplify and improve the judicial process, to ease the public debt and to lower the cost of living.[10]

The Rump Parliament was essentially conservative, the army favoured more radical solutions, Cromwell could not determine what course he wanted. In April 1653 he would dissolve the Rump, and the Long Parliament that had sat for thirteen turbulent years effectively came to an end.

London again 1652–54

In this context Williams and his colleagues made surprisingly good progress. He could report that by October 1652 the Council of State, chaired by Cromwell, had revoked Coddington's charter. The charter of 1644 was reaffirmed—'until further direction and order be given by the Parliament, or this Council.' Coddington was out, but the 1644 charter was not yet unconditionally reaffirmed. Dyer returned to Rhode Island with the news. The colony was fortunate to have men such as Williams and Clarke to represent it. Clarke was a Suffolk man, a few years younger than Williams, a physician, university-educated and a minister. He and Williams remained close until Clarke's death in 1676. Though Williams would return home from the present London trip in 1654, Clarke stayed at his own expense until 1663, when the royal charter was granted.

Meanwhile Williams spent time with Sir Henry Vane, met old friends such as Sir William Masham and Robert Barrington, and spoke frequently with 'Oliver' (Cromwell) himself. He practised with 'some persons ... the Hebrew, the Greek, Latin, French and Dutch.' He taught some Dutch to John Milton and was repaid by a refresher course in 'many more languages.' He entered into correspondence with Sir Edward Coke's daughter, Anne Sadleir, in 1652–53.[11] He wrote of how bitter it was to pass close to her 'deare Father's house on the way to his ship for New England in 1630 without being able to visit him, for I durst not acquaint him with my Conscience and my Flight.' He sent her a copy of his *Experiments of Spiritual Life* but it was returned with her recommendation to read some good royalist and high church literature by King Charles, Richard Hooker, Dr Jeremy Taylor and Bishop Lancelot Andrewes. Never one to take a hint, Williams wrote again, sending her this time a copy of *The Bloudy Tenent, Yet More Bloudy*. She ended her reply to this, 'entreating you to trouble me no more in this kind.' He did trouble her, with concern for her soul. Anne replied, thanking God that her parents had brought her up in 'the old and best religion' it being her 'glorie that I am a member of the church of England.' Williams wrote asking her to read her own Jeremy Taylor—he recommended toleration of all religions. Her last known reply ended with a request to 'trouble me no more with your letters for they are very troublesome to her that wishes you in the place whence you came.' Well, at least he had tried!

Williams wrote to Mary asking her if she could come over. The thought of the voyage was too much for her. He longed to return.

He was waiting to board his ship in March 1654 when he received good news: the Council had decided. The charter of 1644 was at least tacitly though not expressly reaffirmed. John Clarke would remain in London to continue the negotiations. Williams was given another letter warning the United Colonies (Massachusetts, New Haven, Plymouth and Connecticut) not to molest him as he passed through; and a statement of Council policy was made 'that Liberty of Conscience should be maintained at all American Plantations etc.' The declaration had little impact in the colonies.

Experiments of Spiritual Life and Health

While in England, Williams published further works. The first, *Experiments of Spiritual Life and Health* was written while Williams was travelling among the Native Americans in 1650 and he heard that his wife Mary had been seriously ill but had recovered. He wrote a letter to encourage her to attend to the lessons of spiritual health to be learned from physical sickness. At a similar time he received a 'large and pious letter' from Lady Vane. In April 1652 he published the letter to Mary with a dedication to Lady Vane, as *Experiments of Spiritual Life and Health, and their Preservatives, in which the weakest Child of God may get assurance of his Spirituall Life and Blessedness And the strongest may finde proportionable Discoveries of his Christian Growth, and the means of it.'*

This is Williams at his most conventionally Puritan. It is organized under three heads. Under the first he asks what are the evidences of true spiritual life. 'My Dearest Love and Companion in this Vale of Tears,' he begins. Mary's late illness and 'speedy raising' should be taken as, 'a warning from Heaven to make ready for a sudden call to be gone from thence; to live the rest of our short uncertain span, more as strangers, longing and breathing after another Home and Country.' 'My dear Love' he continues—he cannot be with her as much as he would like so he will send her something, 'sweeter than honey and the honeycomb.' This spiritual 'posey' will help her. What are some of the tests of spiritual life? That you know the Lord as Father; that you seek to know him better; that you long after the ordinance of the Word preached; a sincere desire to do that which it cannot do—doing and suffering the will of God; resisting and fighting sin; you will always speak well of God even in affliction; you humbly accept God's hand in affliction; an inclination to enjoy more and more of Christ; restlessness when your relationship with the Lord is broken by sin (Psalm 32); a love of what is seen of Christ in other children of God. In each case Williams distinguishes between the hypocrite and the genuine believer. For example, the hypocrite will say God is her Father, but the child of God cries out to him as Father; the hypocrite may long for more knowledge of God to make use of him, or for the sake of being more knowledgeable, or for the novelty of new knowledge of God, but the child of God will want to know God better for its own sake.

Williams' second head is about how one may tell the strength and vigour of one's spiritual life. For example, when our apprehensions of God are such as to bring us to holy wonderment and amazement at the nature of this incomprehensible God, 'Oh Lord how wonderfull are thy works, in wisdom hast thou made them all' (Psalm 104:24). Secondly, when hallowing God's name is our great work and business; when we do our duty with an eye to God in secret; when prayer is frequent, constant and fervent; when we have a sense of our vileness in God's presence; when our affections are stirring after God as our inheritance; when we have a vehement longing after Christ in visible, open profession of holy worship and ordinances. We see how painful it was for Williams to believe that the true church no longer existed. It was not that he despised the church, far from it; he longed for it; his little groups of believers were a poor substitute for the true church with its ordinances, worship and preaching. Hatred of sin and loathing of self for our sins' sake are signs of spiritual strength; when we use the world as 'if we used it not,' to see God's good pleasure in his withholding or granting material things; when we can control our tongues. He talks about signs of spiritual vigour in relation to others—when we do good to men in order to glorify God; when our hearts melt for the affliction of the miserable; when we resist temptation from one, or accept reproof from another.

His third head is the means of recovering and preserving spiritual strength: self-examination, maintaining an earnest longing after Christ, fellowship with God's people in his ordinances, prayer and fasting. Be careful not to get a 'spiritual cold,' he warns, when our spirits get damp and cold and destitute of Christ's life. Do not surfeit on the world's comforts; meditate on the Word; use afflictions well. Take note of the judgements God has wrought in the earth for the world's sins, how many he has given up 'to those two monstrously bewitching Worships of Mahumatisme [Islam] and Antichristianisme;' but look too to the defeat of these and other enemies and the final victory of Christ.

The abiding paradox of Williams' life was his longing for the community of the church and her ordinances yet believing it was not to be found on earth in his time. He would not settle for anything he considered a poor imitation.

The Fourth Paper Presented by Major Butler

In the spring of 1652, Williams published two more papers arising out of events in England. In December 1648 Colonel Thomas Pride had 'purged' the Long Parliament of members who opposed the execution of the King and the resultant Rump Parliament sat until April 1653. Episcopacy had been replaced by Presbyterianism in 1645; Presbyterianism had been rejected in 1648. Parliament tried to find a solution to the ecclesiastical problem. Caught between those, including many Presbyterian former members of Parliament, who had opposed the execution of Charles I, and the radical groups, led by the Levellers, in the army who sought further reform, the Rump adopted a moderating stance and tried to establish a widely acceptable settlement. A phrase that came into use to describe the way forward was 'the propagation of the gospel.' Initially this meant missionary activity—for example a Society for the Propagation of the Gospel was formed to advance the gospel in New England amongst Native Americans.

But by 1652 the phrase had come to mean something much broader, and included the state regulation and maintenance of tithes for the ministry throughout the nation. This was largely the work of leading Independent ministers. A Committee for the Propagation of the Gospel was set up, Cromwell being one of the members. They prepared fifteen proposals for the 'Furtherance and Propagation of the Gospel in this Nation.'[12] Boards of triers were to be set up to ensure a godly and learned ministry. Preachers would have to be licensed. This would restrict sectarian preaching. Evangelism was to be directed first at the strongholds of royalism in Wales and northern England. Some toleration would be allowed; dissenters would be allowed to meet in places 'publicly known.' Reform was therefore in line with the *Apologeticall Narration* of 1643—it was to be carried out by the 'nursing fathers,' magistrates, with the advice of ministers.

To Presbyterians these proposals already sounded too liberal but they evoked angry responses from the radicals in England. Toleration of this sort, which was as far as the Independents would go, was not the liberty they sought. Major William Butler, an extreme tolerationist and opponent of a state church, submitted a paper to the Committee (the fourth it received, hence the title) making four points against the proposals. Williams published Major Butler's paper with a commentary of his own as a brief but clear summary of his own views. Butler's first and main proposal, with many Scriptures cited in support, was 'whether Christ Jesus, the Lord of the Harvest, doth not send forth Labourers into his Vineyard, furnishing them by his Spirit, and bearing witness to their Labours, without the Testimony and Reward of men?' Christ, not man, calls a minister. It is the Spirit who furnishes a preacher with the credentials and qualifications for preaching. For many Separatists, university learning was not necessary or even proper as a preparation for authentic preaching of the gospel. John Bunyan would have been a case in point, and John Owen is reputed to have told King Charles II that he would have gladly relinquished all his learning had he 'the tinker's abilities' in preaching.

The issue of Spirit endowment over against human learning was a live one. What makes a minister? It is an important question. Williams himself had nothing against learning, but he was sceptical about the value of Cambridge and Oxford educations in preparing a minister. One could of course be called of God and well educated. The problem was that the first of the Committee's fifteen proposals was 'That Persons of Godliness and Gifts, in the Universities and elsewhere, though not ordained, may be admitted to preach the gospel, being approved when they are called thereunto.' Despite the apparent openness the emphasis was on men in the universities; 'mechanick' preachers were not encouraged.

Williams' objections to the Committee's proposals were predictable. It was not up to the civil authority to license preaching. No nation was in the position of Israel; the civil government is still the *civil* government; rulers and governments change—look at the recent history of England; Christ would deal with heretics through the church or in his own way—it was not the government's task:

> Hence, oh that it would please the Father of Spirits to affect the heart of Parliament ... at last to proclaim a true and absolute *Soul-Freedom* to all the people of the land impartially; so that no person be forced to *pray* or *pay* otherwise than as his Soul believes and consents. [Williams' italics]

The Hireling Ministry None of Christ's

Also published in April 1652, this more substantial tract argued that true ministers should not be salaried by the government. Neither Presbyterians nor Independents had any intention of giving up the practice of tithing people to pay for the church. It is Williams' most important work in terms of expounding his views of church and ministry, some of which I explored in Chapter 7. In the first century, Christ sent his apostles into the world, breaking down the barrier between Jew and Gentile. The book of Revelation gives us a panorama of history. From Revelation chapters 6 to 19 we hear no more of the 'white horsemen' (the apostolic ministry), instead only a rout of the church. Therefore there is no true apostolic, converting, ministry today. The church retires into the wilderness of desolation. During this apostasy (of 1260 years)

Christ sends out his prophets and witnesses in sackcloth. Their witness is probably near finished and there will soon be a great persecution and slaughter (Revelation 11). Then they shall rise again. Williams is aware that most interpreters of Revelation 11 see the slaughter of the two witnesses as past but he thinks otherwise.

Is there no church at all on earth now? Only, it appears a would-be church. In *The Bloudy Tenent Yet More Bloudy* Williams concedes that he does acknowledge 'golden candlesticks' (churches) extant but not 'framed after the first pattern'—but they are 'those golden Olive trees and candlesticks, his Martyrs or Witnesses, standing before the Lord' (Revelation 11:4).[13]

Williams gave some personal testimony in *A Hireling Ministry*. He had 'not been altogether a stranger to the Learning of the Aegyptians, and have trod the hopefullest path to Worldly preferments, which for Christ's sake I have forsaken.' He knew what it was to study, to preach, to be an elder, to be applauded, but also what it was to tug at the oar, to dig, to plough, to labour and travel day and night amongst English and Barbarians.

He repeats his views on civil states: they are essentially civil and cannot be called 'Christian.' The civil sword cannot be used in constraining people to worship or restraining them from worship. No-one shall go forth to convert the nations but by the inspiration of the Holy Spirit.

The current ministry of the church he says is defective in four things; firstly, in its gifts; secondly, in its calling, because an apostolic commission was missing; thirdly, in its work, which was involved in a contradiction—pretending to be a ministry to convert people, yet claiming that the English church was already Christian—they were worshipping with the people they professed to be seeking to convert; and fourthly, in its wages. The ministry was a calling, not a trade, he argued. A ministry appointed, licensed and paid by the state, said Williams, was no ministry of Christ's. The sender of a true ministry must be greater than the sent; no civil government is great enough to send a Christian minister.

Would not all ordinances come to an end if the ministry stopped operating? Better that than perpetuate a counterfeit ministry. Two or three Christians can meet in Christ's name for preaching and encouragement; it does not make them a church (which can only be formed with apostolic authority). Those in authority should allow and encourage such true 'volunteers' as give and devote themselves to the service and ministry of Christ Jesus. Further, universities could not make a minister:

> I heartily acknowledge that among all the outward gifts of God, humane learning and the knowledge of languages and good Arts, are excellent ... and therefore that Schools of humane learning ought to be maintained ... yet notwithstanding ... as to the ministry of Jesus Christ ... they will be found to none of Christ's, and that in many respects.[14]

The holy caps, holy gowns and holy scarves of England were far from the purity and simplicity of the Son of God, as far as the attire of a chaste woman was from the 'flaunting vanities of some Painted Harlot.'

As for the duties of magistrates, firstly they should not tax people to support ministers and a religion in which the people did not conscientiously believe; secondly, 'free and absolute permission of the consciences of all men,' should be granted, not excepting even the consciences of Jews, Turks, Papists or Pagans. Such freedom would be a principal means of propagating the gospel in the world.

Williams' great hope was in the return of Christ—when the

ordinances of the church would be restored to their pristine condition. The prophets in sackcloth achieved some good, but they could not restore the primitive church until Christ himself did so. Williams differed from other radicals such as the Fifth Monarchists in his rejection of any civil government promotion of religion—Fifth Monarchists by definition saw an incoming monarchy in the very near future to bring in the kingdom of Christ, replacing the fourth monarchy of world history, the Roman Empire perpetuated through the papacy. Williams also differed from such as Sir Henry Vane in that he looked for the primitive ordinances to be restored, not simply a spiritual kingdom with no visible rites or worship.

The Bloudy Tenent Yet More Bloudy

John Cotton meanwhile had not remained silent. In 1647 he published his riposte to Williams, *The Bloudy Tenent, Washed, and made white in the blood of the Lamb*. In the spring of 1652 Williams replied with *The Bloudy Tenent Yet More Bloudy, By Mr Cotton's endeavour to wash it white in the Blood of the Lamb*—the last salvo in the engagement—because Cotton died in December that year. Had he not, as Edwin Gaustad remarks, 'the argument might have gone on for another thirty years, each convinced of the rectitude of his own position, each convincing the other of very little.'[15] Williams had written the book in about 1649–50 in Rhode Island as he continued to live and trade, bring up a family and keep the lid on various explosive situations in the colony.

Three general points about Williams' *Yet More Bloudy* are worth noting. First, it was after the Parliamentarian victory in the Civil War. Laud and the king were dead. He wanted Parliament to be bold in its embrace of religious toleration—looking to the example of Holland. He defined persecution as restraining people from worshipping the God of whom they are persuaded in their consciences or constraining people to a worship of which they are not persuaded.[16] He cites and refutes five supposed benefits of persecution offered by John Cotton: it puts evil away from the people; the people may hear and fear; it drives wolves away from the sheep; it cures such offenders as are curable; it brings the blessing of God upon the state.[17] He expanded on the duties of a state to treat all equally—summed up in the principle that though a man is not a Christian, 'yet to deprive him of any Civill right or Privilege due to him as a Man, a Subject, a Citizen, is to take from Caesar, that which is Caesar's, which God endures not.'[18] Second, he repeated two of his main points from *The Bloudy Tenent*—Israel was no model for the modern state; civil government is derived from the people. Third, every endeavour should be made to establish the church again as in its pure and primitive New Testament form—its members content to be lowly and poor, the churches purged of the filthiness of false worship, and not persecuting anyone. He concluded the book—even longer than *The Bloudy Tenent*—in a resounding crescendo of twenty-five reasons why persecution for cause of conscience is 'a fowle, black and bloudie Tenent ... a high Blasphemy against the God of Peace.'[19]

Everett Emerson notes that by 1646 there was already dissatisfaction and disillusionment with the Massachusetts colony as the vision faded and unity crumbled. In *The Bloudy Tenent, Washed*, Cotton nonetheless kept his eyes on the ideal, not on the reality. Emerson concludes, echoing a commonly held opinion:

> Williams won the debate; his *Bloudy Tenent* was burned in London ... but the prestige of the New England Way had suffered from the exposé ... The trend of history too was on Williams' side, for when the Holy Commonwealth of Massachusetts Bay became a royal province in 1692, the process of secularisation was complete. Today Williams is viewed as the prophet of the order which was to be.[20]

The Examiner Defended

Finally, in what an editor of Williams' *Complete Writings* calls 'the hectic spring of 1652,' a supporter of toleration, almost certainly Sir Henry Vane, published a work called *Zeal Examined* in favour of freedom of conscience. This was answered by another anonymous author with twenty-two questions in *The Examiner Examined*. Williams responded in September to these questions, also anonymously, on behalf of the first tract, in *The Examiner Defended*. The arguments are familiar. Christ's interest, he asserts, is the Commonwealth's interest and that interest is best served by soul freedom, not oppression. For kings to see themselves as 'nursing fathers' (Isaiah 49:23)—why, is that not just how Charles I saw himself? Did he not feed his wards with poison? Indeed have not most kings? Even if kings are 'nursing fathers' this does not mean spiritual fathers, as Paul described himself in 1 Thessalonians 2. Nor is any man more of a magistrate for being a Christian. The ship he pilots does not bind its passengers to attend ship's prayers—only contribute to the civil peace and common welfare of the vessel. Christ never willed a national church. His teaching contains all we need for the purposes of government. Williams had now come to doubt the validity of baptism by 'dipping' and he abhorred the excesses of such as the Ranters, but is it not also madness to persecute anyone for their conscience? Were not men too wrapped up in national reformations, and their National Models, Platforms, Frames and Forms, so many dead bodies without the life of faith in them?

It was time for Roger Williams to go home.

Chapter 11

Last Battles

TROUBLE AWAITED ROGER WILLIAMS ON HIS RETURN TO PROVIDENCE. One group set itself up as the government of Newport; another claimed Providence and Warwick. Such had been the various quarrels and divisions that before leaving London, Williams had persuaded Sir Henry Vane to write a letter to the town of Providence asking if 'there were no wise men amongst you, no public self-denying spirits that at least upon the grounds of Public Safety, Equity and Prudence can find out some way or means of union and reconciliation?'[1] Providence replied—no doubt prompted by Williams after his return—gratefully and humbly, freed of popish and Anglican ceremonies:

> We have drunk long of the Cup of as great liberty as any people that we can hear of under the whole Heaven ... We have not felt the new chains of the Presbyterian tyrants. Nor in this colony have we been consumed with the overzealous fire of the (so-called) Godly and Christian magistrate.[2]

Williams himself wrote a stern letter to the town reminding

them of criticisms he had borne and his giving up his livelihood to serve the colony in London for two years. It had some effect. By September he had been elected president of the colony, a position he held for three years. He had to write to Massachusetts in the light of deteriorating relationships with the Narragansetts. He organized a Court of Commissioners with representatives of each of the four towns to serve the whole colony. He wrote what is known as his 'ship of state' letter to the town of Providence in January 1655. It gives a clear view of Williams' concept of the relationship between church and state. It also demonstrates something Williams always asserted: he was no anarchist, always believing in civil laws and government and respect for both. At the time certain residents of Providence were objecting to compulsory military service that Williams and others saw as necessary to the welfare of the state. Liberty of conscience he reminded them was not infinite, and he had never said it was:

> There goes many a ship to sea, with many hundred souls in one ship, whose weal and woe is common, and is a true picture of a commonwealth, or a human combination or society. It hath fallen out sometimes that both Papists and Protestants, Jews and Turks, may be embarked in one ship, upon which supposal I affirm, that all the liberty of conscience that ever I pleaded for, turns upon these two hinges: that none of the Papists, Protestants, Jews or Turks be forced to come to the ship's prayers or worship, nor compelled from their own particular prayers or worship, if they practise any. I further add, that I never denied, that notwithstanding this liberty, the commander of this ship ought to command the ship's course, yes, and also command that justice, peace and sobriety be kept and practiced, both among the seamen and all the passengers. If any of the seamen refuse to perform their service, or passengers to pay their freight; if any refuse to help in person or purse towards the common charges or defence; if any refuse to obey the common laws and orders of the ship, concerning their common

peace or preservation; if any shall mutiny and rise up against their commanders and officers, if any should preach or write that there ought to be no commanders or officers, because all are equal in Christ, therefore no masters or officers, no laws, no orders, no corrections, nor punishments; I say I never denied but in such cases, whatever is pretended, the commander and or commanders may judge, resist, compel and punish such transgressors, according to their deserts and merits.[3]

This letter was republished in two works, one of them by Isaac Backus, and widely read at the time of the American War of Independence.

Further pressure on Rhode Islanders to get themselves organized came from Lord Protector ('His Highness' as Williams and others called him now) Oliver Cromwell, probably at the instigation of John Clarke in London, in March 1655. In November, Williams wrote to the Bay Colony to settle a claim for damages owed to Rhode Island. The issue concerning the Pawtuxet land had to be settled. Residents there were evading all responsibilities and taxes by saying they were under Massachusetts' authority. In this letter and again six months later Williams also requested Massachusetts to sell powder and shot to Rhode Island for its defence—a Massachusetts law forbade it. Williams was clearly more concerned about trouble with the Native Americans, arbitration working less well than in the past. He investigated claims that Native Americans had slaughtered two hundred goats belonging to John Winthrop Jr. on Aquidneck Island and found them false, removing a reason for a war of retribution; he held a 'solemn debate' to arbitrate a case where three English sailors had horribly desecrated a Native American grave. Crime was also on the increase; cattle rustling had become a problem.

At a point when Massachusetts seemed to be close to settling the Pawtuxet jurisdiction issue, a delicate case arose. A man

called Richard Chasmore was witnessed by Native Americans in
an act of bestiality with a heifer. This was a crime in any culture.
Because it happened on Pawtuxet land Williams hesitated about
prosecuting the case—lest he should be accused of trespassing
on Massachusetts' authority. Officers from the Bay came to take
Chasmore for trial. Providence men objected. Williams charged
the Providence men, who included his printer and friend Gregory
Dexter, with treason for threatening violence to the Bay officers.
The cases came to court. No witness turned up for the Chasmore
case. He was acquitted. Williams did not give evidence in the
case of the offence against the Bay officers. They were acquitted.
He had made his point. Much as he opposed Massachusetts'
jurisdiction over property that was lawfully Rhode Island's, things
were to be done in a lawful and orderly way. He had not been
Sir Edward Coke's assistant for nothing: legal liberty largely
consists in the due observance of proper procedures. In the next
election, mainly because of these events, being seen to be too
accommodating to Massachusetts, he was not re-elected to office.
In due course Massachusetts abandoned its claim to the area.

Massachusetts had in the previous twenty years banned
Anglicans, antinomians and Baptists from its territory. Now
came the time to ban Quakers. Led in England by George Fox
since 1652, after firm action was taken against their disruptive
behaviour, they were now coming in numbers to the New World.
In 1656 two women tried to preach in Boston. With their doctrine
of 'inner light' which gave them a self-proclaimed authority with
which no-one could argue, they were seen as a real threat to the
Bay and were banished. Still, they persisted. A Quaker woman
walked naked through the streets of Boston; another paraded
naked through a church in Newbury. Banning and forfeiture
of books gave way to floggings. The Bay, however, worried that
Rhode Island would welcome them. They were right. Now without
Williams at the helm the Bay thought they could put pressure on

Rhode Island to prohibit the residence of Quakers. The officers of Rhode Island agreed that Quaker doctrines had disruptive ramifications, and went so far as to say that they would act to 'prevent the bad effects of their doctrines and endeavours.' What they would not do, however (and how Williams, sitting on the sidelines, must have felt a warm inner glow) would be to forbid Quaker worship or to banish the Quakers themselves. 'We have no law among us, whereby to punish for only declaring by words, etc., their minds and understandings concerning the things and ways of God.' Williams' doctrines were bearing fruit.

In 1659 Mary Dyer, wife of the William Dyer who had gone to London with Williams in 1652, was hanged as a Quaker, with three men, in Boston. Floggings and threats had not deterred them—had not Roger Williams warned that persecution only hardens dissidents in their convictions? Quakers flocked to Rhode Island. The United Colonies continued to press: the economic, military and political benefits of membership with them would be open if only Rhode Island prohibited Quaker beliefs and practices. If they did not—sanctions would follow. Once again Rhode Island limited control to civil order; it would not allow 'infringement of that chief principle in our charter concerning freedom of consciences.' How Williams must have rejoiced to see some of his children, at least, walking in the truth.

The royal charter
In England the Rump Parliament had given way in 1653 to the short-lived Barebone's Parliament (a nominated body named after one of its members, the preacher 'Praise-God Barbon') and then to the Lord Protectorate of Cromwell. After the disastrous succession of his son Richard, the army and a now Presbyterian dominated Parliament brought back from exile the son of Charles I who was crowned Charles II in 1660. John Clarke had never left England. He continued to make strenuous efforts on behalf of

Rhode Island, including fighting off claims from the governor of Connecticut, John Winthrop Jr (a close friend of Roger Williams) who had obtained a charter for his colony in 1662 and claimed half of Rhode Island. Nonetheless, in 1663 Charles granted a royal charter to 'Rhode Island and Providence Plantations.' Perhaps Brockunier's conjecture is valid: 'Lord Clarendon and imperial-minded Charles smiled on Rhode Island as a useful offset to the dour intolerance and truculence of New England saints.'[4] The new charter confirmed that 'the form of government established is Democraticall.' A key passage in the lengthy document stipulates:

> Whereas ... they have freely declared, that it is much on their hearts (if they may be permitted) to hold forth a lively experiment, that a most flourishing civil state may stand and best be maintained, and that among our English subjects, with a full liberty in religious concernments ... no person within the said colony, at any time hereafter shall be any wise molested, punished, disquieted, or called in question, for any differences in opinion in matters of religion, and do not actually disturb the civil peace of our said colony.

The charter also affirms that 'true piety rightly grounded upon gospel principles will give the best and greatest security to sovereignty, and will lay in the hearts of men the strongest obligations to true loyalty.' The assumption seems to have been that 'gospel principles' would be at the foundation of the state.

A three-man Royal Commission examined territorial disputes but did not resolve all of them, although by personally appealing to his old friend Major John Mason, now a deputy governor of Connecticut, Williams persuaded Connecticut to drop at least some of its claims. Plymouth maintained some claims, as did Connecticut (to land now comprising Washington County, Rhode Island). Rhode Island's boundaries were not finally fixed until 1747.

John Barry reminds us that 'Williams created the first government in the world which broke church and state apart,' and, 'the only such society [that is, with soul-liberty or universal freedom of conscience] in the civilised world.'[5] One reservation was that voters henceforth had to be not just freeholders (as had been the case since 1658) but of 'competent estates' and of 'civil conversation'—ominous restrictions that would narrow the suffrage in the eighteenth century.

Beloved privacie

Williams, aged sixty-one, writing to John Winthrop Jr., lamented his being called back 'upon the Deck,' from his 'beloved Privacie' to serve in public life. Williams found this mostly at his trading post and among 'my Indian friends' as he called them in one of his letters. He established his trading post at Cocumscussoc, about twenty miles south of Providence, in 1637. Between 1647 and 1651 he built a house there. He traded with Native Americans, English and Dutch in cloth, seed, cooking utensils, tobacco and tools. He refused to sell or buy arms and would only sell strong drink to the Native Americans in small quantities for medicinal purposes. They paid him in furs, skins or baskets which he would sell locally or abroad. Otherwise the Native American 'currency' was 'wampum,' strings of black or white beads which would be used in 'fathoms' in exchange for goods. His old friend Canonicus died in 1647, asking to be buried in cloth from Williams, which Williams freely gave, as he had always freely given much to both Canonicus and Miantonomu; Canonicus had loved him, he said, as a son 'to his last gasp.'

His commercial activity helped to feed his family, his wife Mary and six children. His first daughter, Mary, was born in Plymouth in 1633 and his second, Freeborn, in Salem in 1635. His other four children were born in Providence: a son, Providence, in 1638, Mercy in 1640, Daniel in 1641 and Joseph in 1643. Mary died in 1676, and all their children survived Williams. The trading post also gave him time to be quiet, to get away from the contentions of political life, time to write (for example, *The Bloudy Tenent Yet More Bloudy* and *Experiments of Spiritual Life*) and to correspond with friends, like John Winthrop Jr, frequently governor of Connecticut from the late 1650s. The older Winthrop had died in 1649 and had become increasingly cool towards Williams as the years went by. But the friendship with Winthrop Jr was a genuine and enlivening one for both men, involving exchange of books and pamphlets and surviving even Connecticut's later claims on the Narragansett territory of Rhode Island.

Williams' spirituality can be seen in the book he wrote for Mary to encourage her after a time of affliction, but it is evident in the letters he wrote in a much more natural way than his published works. All Puritans naturally referred events in their lives to God and interpreted everything in public and private life as from his hand in blessing or chastisement. You can barely read more than a few lines of any Williams letter without coming across a reference to God or to the Bible in some way. For example, in 1670 he wrote the letter referred to above to Major John Mason concerning the Connecticut land dispute. He devoted a whole paragraph to the spiritual aspects of such disputes:

> Alas, Sir, (in calm midnight thoughts) what are these leaves, and flowers, and smoke and shadows and dreams of earthly nothings about which we poor fools and children, as David says, disquiet ourselves in vain? Alas what is all the scuffling of this world for? ... How much sweeter is the counsel of the Son of God, to mind first the matters of his kingdom? To take no care for tomorrow?[6]

Land had become the English 'god,' he wrote ruefully. In a letter in December 1648 to Winthrop Jr., from Cocumscussoc, he plays on the parallel of a candle and his physical and spiritual life:

Our candle burns out day and night. We need not hasten its end by swaling [the sputtering end of a candle's life] in unnecessary miseries: unless God call us for him [Jesus] to suffer whose our breath is, and hath promised, to such as hate life for him, an eternal [life].[7]

For Williams, writes Edwin Gaustad:

Religion had to be of the heart, not just of the mind—of direct, transforming experience, not 'the Favor or Custom of any Men or Times'. In other words, Williams was a pietist, one who counted the presence of God in his life as more valuable than all the world's riches and honors.[8]

In the later 1660s land struggles continued, notably with William Harris who kept making claims for more. But these quarrels were soon eclipsed in an all-consuming crisis. Rumours of Native plotting against the English were flying thick and fast. Williams investigated them, on one occasion even gave himself as a hostage to the Wampanoags to assure the safe return of their sachem, Philip, from Plymouth. Williams again showed his relentless perseverance as a peacemaker, in negotiation, in patient investigation of claim, accusation and counterclaim, in the interest of both settler and Native in New England. The man who had shown tactlessness and argumentativeness with the Puritan authorities in his youth, and who had been called by John Cotton a man of 'self-conceited, and unquiet, and unlamblike frame,' repeatedly demonstrated himself to be without peer in patient and persuasive negotiation, mediation and arbitration in pursuit of peace.

Alas, this time, the forces rumbling towards war overwhelmed even his skills.

In 1675 a Native American who had been converted informed Plymouth that Philip was preparing for war. For that betrayal he was murdered. Tensions mounted as three men were charged with the murder. Williams tried to dissuade the Narragansetts from joining with Philip in any war. But nine Englishmen were murdered in Swansea, Massachusetts. 'Sir my old bones and eyes are weary with travel and writing to the governors of Massachusetts and Rhode Island and now to yourselves,' Williams wrote in June 1675 to Winthrop Jr, 'I end with humble cries to the Father of Mercies to extend his ancient and wonted mercies to New England.'[9]

On 24 June 1675 what has become known as King Philip's War broke out, the Native American tribes in league with each other. Fifty-two of New England's ninety towns were attacked, Warwick and Providence being among the dozen or so destroyed or nearly so. About 600 English were killed, and many more Native Americans killed or, after the war, sold into slavery. The war ended in August. Native American power was broken. Had such a war happened in 1636, when Williams drew the sting of the Native American alliance, it is likely the English would have been driven into the sea. Williams' home was destroyed, along with 100 of 120 in the town, but he had removed his family onto Aquidneck Island where they would be safe through the war. During the war, and in his seventies, he stayed in Providence as a captain to protect lives and property.

Debating with Quakers

Meanwhile Williams had been fighting battles of a more familiar kind. Liberty of conscience in Rhode Island had brought Baptists, antinomians, mystics and others. Jews came, especially from Holland and Spain's American colonies; in 1658 fifteen families arrived and established the first Hebrew congregation under the English flag in Newport. Cotton Mather called Newport, 'the common receptacle of the convicts of Jerusalem and the outcasts of the land.' 'Receptacle' was a favourite term of abuse for Rhode

Island.[10] From the late 1650s Rhode Island particularly attracted Quakers. By 1661 they could hold a 'Yearly Meeting' at Newport. The Quaker founding of Pennsylvania was still two decades away. In 1672 a Quaker was elected governor of Rhode Island. In that same year their leader, George Fox, visited Newport. People, it seems, were being bitten by the 'infectious teeth' of the Quakers. Roger Williams challenged him to a debate. He set out fourteen propositions to be discussed. The debate took place over three days in August 1672 in Newport, with a fourth day in Providence. Unfortunately, for whatever reason, Fox had left too soon to get the letter so Williams was left debating three of his followers.

Williams paddled himself the twenty miles or so along Narragansett Bay from Providence to Newport. He was sixty-nine. It is reminiscent of his journey to parley with the Pequots and Narragansetts in 1636. He might have preferred that to debating the Quakers.

Why did he do it? Was his enthusiasm for freedom of conscience cooling off? Perish the thought. No Quaker was ever arrested, fined, whipped or hanged for their beliefs in Rhode Island. They were never banished or prevented from entering the colony. Williams insisted on their right to live in the colony but he did not agree with their beliefs. His commitment to liberty of conscience was not out of indifference to the truth but out of passion for it. He believed the Quakers had a right to live in the land even if they were wrong in their beliefs, and even if they propagated those beliefs. If they transgressed civil law—by outrageous behaviour, as they had frequently done elsewhere—that was a different matter. But they had a right to their beliefs, humanly speaking, even if they were wrong. Williams, meanwhile, had a right to challenge them about their beliefs and try to persuade them of their errors. There is hardly a more potent symbol of his commitment to both truth and peace than the old man rowing over the waters to Newport to engage in this contest. Teresa Bejan argues that:

> His determination to tolerate the Quakers in Rhode Island, despite his personal contempt for them, should be seen as a powerful illustration of what true toleration—as the willingness to coexist with those people and views one finds most contemptible—really looks like.[11]

Quakers believed that the spirit that had been in the apostles now dwelt in the 'Children of Light.' The final authority in faith and experience was therefore not Scripture, as with Puritans, but the dictates of the spirit or 'light' within. Williams' first proposition against them was that they were not 'true Quakers according to the Holy Scriptures'—that is, they were not people who trembled at God's Word and worked out their salvation with fear and trembling, but were proud, strangers to truly spiritual pious and civil behaviour. Instead of God's guidance they placed their reliance on themselves. Such reliance on the spirit within led them away from Christ to belief in the perfection of the individual based on union with Christ. They 'preached not Christ Jesus but themselves.' His second proposition was therefore that the Christ, the 'Christ within' who was everything, whom they professed, was not the true Christ; the third was that their 'spirit' was not the Spirit of God; the fourth, that they did not own the Holy Scriptures. The propositions continued: their religion was a confusion of Arminianism, Socinianism, Popery and Judaism; their doctrines were full of contradictions, hypocrisies and heresies; the Pope did not swell with pride as much as the Quakers did; and their religion (hardly surprisingly, if all this was true) was destructive of the conversion and salvation of souls.

Williams was someone to whom, as he had once written, in August 1651, to John Winthrop Jr., 'That word Literall [the Bible] is sweet, as it is the Field, where the misticall Word or Treasure

Christ Jesus lies hid.'[12] The saint must evaluate his experience by the Bible. Nor could Williams abide the Quakers' rejection of the sacraments. His lifelong desire was to see the church and sacraments restored in their purity. He had no time for a new or future age of the spirit where the visible ordinances would be superfluous. When criticized by the Quakers for 'not living in church ordinances' (a valid criticism one might have thought) Williams' reply was that it was one thing to be in opposition to Christ and his visible kingdom (as he alleged the Quakers were), but quite another, in the midst of so many pretenders, to be uncertain (as Williams claimed he was) as to which to associate himself with.

Quaker reliance on the spirit led to their uncivil behaviour—bodily quaking, nudity in public, excessive fasting. When the Quakers claimed such behaviour was a sign from God they were, in effect, saying that they were constrained by divine power. If that was the case, reasoned Williams, it was by the devil's power not the Holy Spirit.

The debate drew out of Williams some corrections of previous imbalances though not any change of position. He now asserted the benefit of human learning and knowing Hebrew and Greek, against the Quakers' contempt for such things; he qualified the call of the Spirit to ministry by insisting that God worked through means—the Word in some way—though he allowed that God may occasionally work through dreams or meditations, not only in sermons or public reading of Scripture.

By the end of the first day they had not finished the first proposition. They made better progress on day two, a Saturday. Williams read out passages from and, to his satisfaction at least, demolished, George Fox's book *The Great Mystery of the Great Whore unfolded; and Anti-Christ's Kingdom revealed unto Destruction*, published in 1659. He suffered from a severe headache and a hoarse voice but 'the Lord graciously carried me through the whole day with little hindrance to myself and little disadvantage to the understanding of the Auditors'—who included the Quaker governor, Nicholas Easton. Williams complained of rudeness and interruptions, and by the end of day two only two propositions had been completed. He promised to limit himself to fifteen minutes each on propositions three to seven on day three—Monday. Day four was Friday, in Providence. One of Williams' last arguments was the most hard-hitting: Quakers had never been truly converted. 'Till a spirit of Regeneration and Conversion change the heart of a man, there is no other Christ nor Spirit within, but the spirit of Satan, which is the spirit by which the Quakers are acted,' he said.

Williams had rarely sounded so Puritan—mainstream Puritan, that is. He wrote up the debates in his last book, *George Fox Digg'd out of his Burrowes*—a play on the name of another Quaker leader, Edward Burrough. Massachusetts, who must have smiled wryly at the vision of Williams going hammer and tongs with heretics, actually liked his book. For the first time Roger Williams had a book published in Boston, in 1676, and governor John Leverett agreed to meet the expenses.

This peculiar debate is fascinating in that it made Williams distance himself from a religious group who were more unorthodox than he was. Up to now, he had been pitching his arguments against the establishment. Now we see his commitment to the pillars of more orthodox beliefs—Scripture, God's use of means, the importance of visible ordinances, the inadequacy of an 'inner Christ' who was not also an historical Christ. These were not a change of position for Williams; but debating the Quakers made Williams assert them clearly.

There was one final publication. It saw the light for the first time in 2014. An English Baptist minister, John Norcott, wrote a defence of believer's baptism in 1672; John Eliot replied to it in 1679; Williams responded to Eliot, defending believer's baptism, in about 1680. Because of the paper shortage he wrote his reply in shorthand in the margins of another book in his library. This book came to rest in the John Carter Brown library in Providence, Rhode Island. In 2011–12 the shorthand was eventually decoded revealing the book called *A Brief Reply to a Small Book Written by John Eliot*. This last work of Williams has now been published by the translators as *Decoding Roger Williams* with an introductory essay, editorial notes, and the full texts of the books by Norcott and Eliot.

As to the content—the argument for believer's baptism is conventional enough, interesting not so much for the substance but for the reminder that Williams still believed in believer's baptism four decades after he had stopped worshipping in a Baptist church. His brief comments on Native American conversion, in response to arguments made by Eliot in his book, are more significant to issues in Williams' life and are referred to in the Appendix.

Last days

In a letter to John Winthrop Jr. during King Philip's War in 1675, Williams wrote, 'Why is our Candle burning but to glorify our dreadful former [that is, our wonderful Creator, God] and in making our calling and election sure, and serving God, in serving the public in our generation.'[13] That willingness to serve God by serving 'the public' sums up much that was central to Roger Williams. He wanted to separate from spiritual impurity but not from people; he saw more danger in the impure church than in wholehearted engagement with the world—the dirty world too, of politics and war. He had served as his colony's 'First Officer' from 1644–47 and President from 1654–56 as well as assistant or deputy

on various occasions, yet there was never any hogging of power—
he was reluctant to take up the reins but did so when called.

In his last years, the Connecticut claims continued over the
Narragansett territory; William Harris continued to assert claims
to Pawtuxet. He died in 1681 but the dispute continued into
the next century. Still writing letters, having to beg for paper,
Williams continued 'in serving the public' to the end. In 1680 he
wrote to the town of Providence reminding them of the necessity
of paying rates. In 1682 he wrote to Massachusetts governor
Simon Bradstreet (husband of poet Anne) asking if he could see
to the publishing of twenty-two sermons for him—sermons he
had preached to 'the scattered English at Nahigonset before the
war and since.' That his preaching was appreciated in later years
as well as in his youth is seen from a 1673 letter from Richard
Smith Jr. to Winthrop Jr., when Winthrop Jr. had offered to send
a preacher to Wickford. 'Mr Williams does exercise amongst us,'
he was informed, 'and he preaches well and ably, and much people
come to hear him to their good satisfaction.'[14]

The sermons he sent to Bradstreet have not survived; their titles
have though, for example: 'Of Atheisme'; 'Of the holy Scriptures';
'Of the Sower and his 4 sorts of Ground'; Of the goulden Chaine
of Predestination Vocation Justification and Glorification'; 'Of
Eternitie'; 'Mistakes about Christianitie'; 'the drowning of the Old
World'; 'Jobs Trialls and Patience'; 'Considerations on the Lily'.[15]

'Eternitie, (O Eternitie) is our Busines..." were virtually the
last words we have from his hand, written to Simon Bradstreet
in 1682.[16] Williams' end came sometime in early 1683. No-one
knows the exact date. He was buried in the hillside behind where
his home had stood. One witness remembered that muskets
were fired over his grave. He died a poor man, 'He gave away
his lands and other estate to them that he thought were most
in want, until he gave away all,' wrote his son Daniel in 1710.[17]

A Providence town record refers to 'The Venerable remains of Mr Roger Williams, the Father of Providence, the Founder of the Colony, and of Liberty of Conscience.' Cotton Mather, who opposed Williams' convictions, later wrote:

> It was more than forty years after his exile that he lived [in Rhode Island], and in many things acquitted himself so laudably, that many judicious persons judged him to have had the 'root of the matter' in him, during the long winter of his retirement: He used many commendable endeavours to Christianize the Indians in his neighbourhood, of whose language, tempers and manners he printed a little relation with observations ... There was always a good correspondence always held between him and many worthy and pious people in the colony, from whence he had been banish'd, tho' his keeping still so many of his dangerous principles kept the government, unto whose favour some of the English nobility had by letter recommended him, from taking off the sentence of his banishment. And against the Quakers he afterwards maintained the main principles of the Protestant religion with much vigour in some disputations.[18]

In 1936 the Commonwealth of Massachusetts deemed his principles less dangerous, and revoked the order of exile.

Chapter 12

Conscience

IN ORDER TO PUT WILLIAMS' THINKING INTO THE CONTEXT OF ISSUES facing contemporary western society, and particularly what might typically be thought of as Christian culture, the next three chapters will address three questions. First, is liberty of conscience something we should treasure and protect? Second, what should the relation be between church and state? Third, how important is religion to the existence and stability of a society?

The Protestant conscience

When Martin Luther proclaimed at the Diet of Worms 'My conscience is captive to the Word of God. I cannot and will not recant anything, for to go against conscience is neither safe nor right,' he was establishing a fundamental principle of Protestantism—passionate concern for a clear conscience. It has two elements: first, attachment to Scripture as the supreme authority for belief and conduct; second, that conscience must be obeyed.

The Puritans, following Luther but more particularly Calvin, developed a highly sophisticated theology of the conscience. William Ames defined conscience as, 'A man's judgment of himself according to the judgment of God on him.'[1] Puritans, including Roger Williams, taught that conscience is universal—all people have a conscience. It is ineradicable; it is authoritative; and it is rational because it understands what God's will is and declares it to us and judges actions by it. Conscience is a medium between God and man. It is God's instrument for aligning human thought and behaviour with his mind. It is not itself revelation or law—the requirements of which are written in every human heart (Romans 2:14–15)—but it declares and applies it to us. It operates according to God's law in creation—what we call natural revelation, available to all people; and in his Word—special revelation. It is God's witness and ambassador in the soul reminding us of our responsibility to God and instructing us how to think and live. Conscience therefore performs several functions: it is a register of our thoughts, words and actions; the accuser of what is wrong and the approver of what is right.

In a perfect world conscience would function perfectly but in a fallen world conscience fails to register our actions accurately; it does not correctly condemn what is wrong, nor adequately approve what is right. Yet it is still God's agent (though not strictly speaking his 'voice') in the soul and Luther is biblical and right to say that it is 'neither safe nor right' to go against it. The fallen conscience may direct you to do what is wrong—like the man in Rhode Island who according to conscience (at least so he claimed) forcibly prevented his wife going to church. At some point the authorities have a duty to prevent wrongdoing (when it becomes a crime) and such prevention may transgress conscience. It is true to say that we should be at least as concerned to educate conscience according to the Bible as to obey conscience. Nonetheless the general principle is that conscience should be obeyed. Obeying the corrupt conscience may lead to sin but disobeying conscience is sin and is tacit contempt for God, for it is still God's messenger we are disobeying.

Williams and Cotton

Roger Williams spoke of conscience in familiar terms as the 'candle of the Lord' in the human heart. He defined it most fully as:

> A persuasion fixed in the mind and heart of a man, which enforceth him to judge (as Paul said of himself a persecutor) and to do so and so, with respect to God, his worship., etc. This conscience is found in all mankind, more or less, in Jews, Turks, Papists, Protestants, Pagans, etc.[2]

By 'persuasion' Williams shows that the mind is involved. It operates according to reason. He has particular regard to its workings in matters relating to God and worship, though he does not deny its functions in all of life. In making Rhode Island a haven for those 'distressed for conscience' he was expressing the conviction that God alone should be recognized as Lord of the conscience.

He was not of course the first to recognize that the conscience cannot be forced in matters of religion. Lactantius, tutor to the son of the emperor Constantine, asserted in the fourth century that 'religion is, first and foremost, a matter of free will, and no man can be forced under compulsion to adore what he has no will to adore.' The Puritans under James and Charles in England had asserted it and suffered for it. What was different about Williams was his consistent advocacy and practice of insisting on freedom of conscience for everybody. As Francis Wayland, president of Brown University, Providence, said in 1860, the Pilgrims in America (and he might have added, the Puritans in England) sought liberty for themselves; Roger Williams sought 'liberty for humanity.'[3]

John Cotton asserted that no man should be persecuted for conscience. Fair enough. But he argued that in fundamental principles of doctrine and worship the Bible was so clear that a person could not but be convinced in conscience of the dangerous error of his way.[4] Cotton was well within Puritan thinking in insisting that the commands of Scripture, properly interpreted by wise and godly men, must take precedence over the erring individual conscience. You can, however, see what Cotton's logic implies. First, that only a Christian confessing orthodoxy as currently defined can have a good conscience; second, to hold to your beliefs when they disagree with such orthodoxy is not to be *conscientious* but to sin against your conscience; and third, to have a good conscience you have to follow the teachings of orthodoxy even if you are convinced they are wrong.

For Williams, however, mind and will must act together; one cannot safely deny what one believes with the mind, by acting against it by the will. His idea of conscience is much more to do with the mind; Cotton's is to do with the will. Cotton's focus was on *doing* what is right, according to God's law (which tended to equate to current orthodoxy) even when not convinced of it, and being prepared to go against what one believes, because after all, the individual doing so is wrong to believe what they believe. Williams is convinced that the conscience should remain inviolate and is convinced too of the futility of forced belief. His insistence on engaging in debate with people, his preference for arbitration of disputes, his remarkable patience in negotiation and his persistence in reasoning with those with whom he disagreed, are not only born of his Puritanism, but testimony to his belief in the possibility and importance of persuasion rather than force.

Resolving the tension between the absolute demands of divine law and the erroneous conscience is not easy. Despite the views held by Cotton the Puritans in general advised that conscience was to be followed because it was God's deputy in the soul, and even if it could be wrong it was never safe to go against conscience. 'Whatsoever a man does,' wrote William Perkins, 'whereof he is not certainly persuaded in judgment and conscience out of God's Word, that the thing may be done, *it is sin*.' As an example, 'an Anabaptist, that holds it unlawful to swear, sins if he takes an oath: not in swearing simply, for that is God's ordinance, but because he swears against the persuasion of his conscience.'[5] If an erroneous conscience leads you to sin (for example you think bigamy is morally permissible or even compulsory) you sin by the act but not against conscience; if you commit adultery knowing it is wrong, you sin doubly, against the law and against conscience. Rebellion against what you believe to be God's voice (even if your belief is wrong) reveals contempt for God; the remedy is to align conscience more and more with the Word of God.

Williams, says James Calvin Davis, was familiar with the Puritan writings of Perkins and Ames but was unlike the Massachusetts Puritans in his unwillingness to surrender freedom of conscience even in the cause of supposed doctrinal purity.

'As it did for Thomas [Aquinas], Calvin, Perkins and Ames,' says Davis, 'the evaluative function of conscience in Williams' thought depended on the natural law.'[6] Conscience is a judgement in the soul in which a person's actions and beliefs are evaluated according to the standards of natural morality (that is, the law of God written in the heart). His *A Key* was largely a comparative analysis of Native American culture with English customs and behaviour. He believed that the Native Americans showed real respect for conscience, sometimes more than the English and they also showed more respect for variations in conscience than he observed in his own society. 'There is a savour of civility and courtesy even amongst these wild Americans, both amongst themselves and towards strangers,' he wrote.[7]

Conservative and liberal views

The dominant spirit in Massachusetts was of the conservative Reformed strand that valued conformity to institutional authority over allegiance to individual conscience. Richard Baxter was typical of such a view, 'Liberty in all matters of Worship and of Faith, is the open and apparent way to set up Popery in the land.'[8] Williams may be said to represent the liberal or left wing of the tradition, arguing that conscience is what makes human beings, even 'natural man' capable of basic morality and sociability. His convictions about conscience not only paved the way for freedom of belief but justified the possibility of civil government amongst people of very different religious beliefs or of none.

A representative of the more conservative view was the Scottish Presbyterian Samuel Rutherford, who wrote, in *A Free Disputation against Pretended Liberty of Conscience*, what Owen Chadwick called, 'the ablest defence of persecution during the seventeenth century.'[9] Rutherford gives a clear, typically Puritan account of the nature and workings of conscience. His main target however is the subjectivism of the sects and men like Williams (whose writings are criticized specifically in the book) and John Milton, who elevated personal conviction above what Rutherford saw as the clarity of Scripture. He agrees that religion is a matter of the heart and conversion cannot be forced by the sword. He does not want to interfere with the inner liberty to think, understand and conclude. Yet he is contemptuous of the views of such as Cromwell that conscience is inviolable and is thus made 'every man's Rule, Umpire, Judge, Bible and his God.' He insists that Scripture is clear, if interpreted properly, and that there is no excuse for maintaining deviant opinions. Conscience, to be good, has to combine a good will and right understanding. The fallen conscience is badly flawed; its judgements are only to be trusted as long as they are subordinate to God's law written in the human heart and in Scripture which republished and clarified that law. You are not to follow it, therefore, if it transgresses Scripture. But who is to interpret Scripture to elicit its true meaning? Ministers and synods, says Rutherford.

For punishment there was, as well as church disciplines, recourse also to the magistrate and his 'sword.' Basing his arguments on the Old Testament and bolstering them with reference to Augustine's use of force against the Donatists, Rutherford justifies the magistrate in acting against apostates from the faith though only if they actively propagated their blasphemies. The sword can lawfully punish external (not internal) acts of worship, he argues, so far as those acts are seen by men and are destructive to the souls of Christians.

In essence, the argument is that false prophets must be punished to protect society from heresy. It was the argument of John Cotton, the argument of the sacral state, or the Christian state, with Old Testament Israel as its model.

Conscience and the common good

Williams would have fundamentally disagreed with Rutherford about the state's role in religious matters and objected principally to coercion—the 'bloudy tenent of persecution' as he put it—which he saw as inseparable from state involvement in the church. One may *be right*, but one does not have the right to force that on others in matters of religion nor stop them living by or proclaiming their views, provided civil order is not offended. There lies the rub, of course, and Williams discovered the difficulty of marking the boundary of 'civil order' with consistency. He knew that a successful state needed to distinguish between liberty and licence and rebuked some of his fellow

Rhode Islanders for pursuing the latter. Law-breaking had to be punished. Human sacrifice and prostitution, and the naked appearances of Quakers, were practices sometimes justified by religion but which a civil government should prohibit. He would have prohibited long hair for men, condemning the fashion of 'the monstrous hair of women, upon the heads of some men'—a moral offence he attributed to the forgetting of nature.[10]

On the other hand he indicated that he did not think it right to impose even Christian morality (let alone the Christian religion) as a system—he clearly held to the Christian framework but was willing to concede that differences could be valid and tolerated. For example, the divorce laws in Rhode Island were the most liberal in New England—perhaps reflecting the influence of John Milton on Williams. In James Calvin Davis' summary of Williams, there have to be laws to maintain civil society but coercing conscience illegitimately will morally bankrupt society. Davis also refers to Thomas Aquinas' view, similar to Williams', that conscience can be made to err by being deprived of the free use of reason and choice it needs to operate with integrity. Oppression leaves consciences immature. For the public good, a person may have to be coerced against conscience (say a man conscientiously believed in polygamy or prostitution) but this would still be a violation, albeit justified.

By his own struggles in this area Williams demonstrated that there was room for difference of opinion, but he also made clear his conviction that conscience alone was not sufficient justification for behaviour injurious to the public welfare.

It must be remembered that Williams allowed for no exceptions to his principle. John Locke would not allow atheists liberty of conscience because they would not take an oath which was regarded as essential to the stability of society; neither would Locke allow Roman Catholics liberty as they owed allegiance to a foreign power (the papacy). Williams did allow a concession to the state in relation to Roman Catholics—they might be required to wear distinctive clothing. But they would not be forced to worship against their will, nor prevented from worshipping according to their convictions.[11] James D. Knowles concluded, 'Roger Williams is entitled to the honor of being the first writer, in modern times, who clearly maintained the absolute right of every man to a "full liberty in religious concernments."'[12]

Conscience, personal integrity and the west today

What about today? It is often assumed that respect for conscience is a given of civilized life and of western liberal democracy in particular. But where does it come from? Larry Siedentop makes a powerful case for the moral equality of human beings being the central tenet of western civilization and Christianity being the source of that principle.[13] Man is made in the image of God and this makes him inviolable except by proper authority on duly justified occasions. This principle leavened western society through the influence of the church and came to fruition in the early modern era. Respect for conscience is a necessary corollary of such moral equality—it is the recognition of it in practice. But in the Middle Ages and under the papacy it had little place. In Christendom after the fourth century moral equality in practice was only for orthodox Christians. The free conscience came into its own in the Reformation as the recovery of the doctrine of justification by faith alone gave individuals access to God apart from the institutional church. The conscience, as Luther's famous speech indicates, took centre stage. Yet the medieval mind-set clung on. It took another century after Luther for the idea of the free conscience in religion to find its voice. Williams was one of its most significant voices.

The Christian worldview has now long lost its power over the western mind. However the reality is that despite many secular attempts to justify the principle of 'moral equality' it has not been done satisfactorily. Raymond Plant, Professor of Jurisprudence and Political Philosophy at King's College, London, asks the salient question, 'What is it that gives liberalism such authority and why are its beliefs and values so privileged?'[14] He acknowledges the importance of Christianity in developing principles of human dignity, but tries then to distance those principles from the Christian faith. He sets out (though is not basing his argument on) a number of reasons why it could be argued that liberalism should be privileged—it is based on consent, not force; it values reasonableness; it is the best way of coping with stresses in society, etc. But these are descriptions of some of the benefits of liberalism rather than justifications for its primacy over, say, fundamentalist religious views held by some in society.

In a way, this is the best a secular approach can do. Jocelyn Maclure and Charles Taylor argue for two central values or ends for society—equality of respect (moral equality) and freedom of conscience.[15] As means to achieve those ends, they specify the separation of church and state and 'the state's religious neutrality,' thereby respecting pluralism. But where do those values come from? Maclure and Taylor surmise that different religions or philosophical positions will derive them from different sources— Christians from creation in God's image, a rationalist from the necessity to recognize the equal dignity of human beings, a utilitarian from the need to maximize the happiness of the majority of sentient beings and a Buddhist from a principle of non-violence. We might respond: none except the Christian approach gives a reason derived from the unique nature of what a human being is. No other belief has proved as enduring or as fruitful across the centuries and across cultures. In the end, no other will do, no other root will provide the fruit.

We are living, as Williams realized he was, in 'wonderful

searching, disputing, and dissenting times.'[16] Men and women such as the authors of the above books are trying to find ways for us to live together in peace. One need not argue for what is called liberalism in all its aspects but Christians should value liberty of conscience. Os Guinness speaks of the three fundamental freedoms—of conscience, speech and assembly.[17] Conscience is the foremost. The other two presuppose it. First, it is important because a man is bound by it—it is where you say, 'Here I stand, I can do no other.' Second, freedom of conscience is the key to civil society and social harmony. We need to be able to combine strong religious convictions with strong political liberty.

We value liberty of conscience for the sake of individuals, for the sake of the church, and for the sake of society. We value it for the gospel's sake, the bringing in of the kingdom of God, his reign and lordship over individuals, the church and the world. We value it because God's Word is truth and he applies it to hearts not by force but by his Word and his Spirit. Of the arguments for liberty of conscience we listed in discussing *The Bloudy Tenent*, the fundamental one for Williams was that God alone is Lord of the conscience.

Further, if we value liberty of conscience there is no firm basis but the Christian doctrine of man. Williams did not have to argue for that but he did show us its significance for freedom in society. It means freedom of conscience for everybody. Moreover he knew that when not everyone agreed with him he had to be ready to persuade. We can work with people who hold substantially the same views as we do in civil and political matters even if not from the same basis. We do not have to be ashamed of our foundation but it does not have to be explicit in working with others. We can present the case that if you separate the root from the fruit you will in the end lose the latter. We can also persuade directly in the right time and place of the significance of the roots—biblical Christianity—and maybe some will listen.

Chapter 13

Church and State

THE SECOND QUESTION I WANT TO CONSIDER IN RELATION TO
contemporary society is: what should be the proper relationship
between the church and the state? We have seen above that this
issue is inseparable from freedom of conscience. It is in relation to
human freedom that the reality of state control is most keenly felt.
Yet the question is a bigger one. It is about how Christ governs the
world and the church. He is head of both but the church alone is
his body (Ephesians 1:22–23). The world is under Christ's authority
for the sake of the church. Every authority is ordained by God and
Christians are under obligation to obey (Romans 13:1–7).

Williams would have denied none of this. In a letter to
Providence in 1682 he gave a list of reasons why the residents
should pay taxes: government and order is the Ordinance of the
Most High for the peace and good of mankind; government is
one of the things written on the hearts of all mankind; there is
no man anywhere who does not submit to government; either we
must have justice prevail through courts or the 'law of arms' must

prevail; it is better to live under a tyrant in peace than under the sword (where everyone is a tyrant).[1]

Yet he fought for the separation of church and state to a degree unknown before and established a government unique in its time but quickly and often copied thereafter, not least by the United States of America in the First Amendment.

The historical background

The relationship between the state and the institutional church has been a matter of debate since Constantine ended official persecution of the church in the Roman Empire in the fourth century. After his successors made Christianity the official religion of the Empire, the principal model became that of the 'two swords,' the priests on the one hand, the emperor on the other, the emperor subservient to the church in spiritual matters, the church to the emperor in political matters. In the Middle Ages the Catholic Church saw itself as the soul, the state as the body, and soon argued that the soul should take precedence in all things as the soul did in the body. With the rise of nation states there were conflicts between the Pope and monarchs culminating in the tearing of power away from the Pope in the sixteenth century. Henry VIII did this politically, and Martin Luther, far more radically and effectively, theologically.

The Lutheran, Reformed and, in England, Anglican churches, however, maintained a similar outlook on the relationship of church and state as soul and body; 'twins' was a favourite metaphor of the Puritans to describe the relationship. They were distinct but helped one another, working in harmony in their respective spheres. The Puritans of course knew that the reality was often very different, but this relationship of co-operation is what they hoped to establish in New England. What they set up has been described as more of a separation between church and state than was known in any part of Europe at that time.

As we have seen, this was not enough for Roger Williams. His driving principle was liberty of conscience. He wanted to worship purely—with no taint of the Anglican church which all in New England agreed was corrupt but opinions differed on how separate they should be. Williams wanted total separation, not only of the churches from the mother church but of the church from the state. He wanted to build a state where people would be free to worship according to conscience and he saw that this had to be one where the state had no authority over the souls of men.

Williams' arguments

His argument began with the freedom of conscience that God has permitted; idolatry and error are only to be fought against by the Word and Spirit not by secular force. He argued that although government is an ordinance of God, all civil states are essentially civil and are not competent in spiritual matters; the particular ruler's authority derives from the people; the church must not be placed under the world. Spiritual gifts, offices and weapons are sufficient to deal with spiritual enemies; the church does not need the state either to establish or preserve churches. State interference in the church, Williams concluded, will lead to the church becoming a wilderness.

His main target in the Puritan context was the model of Old Testament Israel. Williams is clear that Israel's role was fulfilled in the coming of Christ: 'The state of the land of Israel, the kings and people thereof, in peace and war, is proved figurative and ceremonial, and no pattern nor precedent for any kingdom or civil state to follow.'[2] Use of the Old Testament therefore to justify punishment by the state of heretics, blasphemers or unbelievers, or to force people to go to church by law or to restrict civil office to church members, all of which was done in Massachusetts, was illegitimate, said Williams.

The basic principle of separation was the difference between his vision and that of Winthrop. John Barry writes, 'Williams saw the individual standing alone with God … Winthrop saw a state committed to Christian ideals, demanding conformity and imposing community standards upon individuals.'[3] Winthrop saw the state as a 'foster father' to the church. Williams responded that government is a creation ordinance, known amongst pagans as well as among Christians; when the state is asked to look after the church, it inevitably happened in history 'by degrees that the gardens of churches of the saints were turned into the wilderness of whole nations.'[4] The effect of Christianity becoming the official imperial religion was looked upon by Williams as a disaster for the church. Williams was realistic; give the government authority over the church and anything could happen. He did allow that the government should encourage and protect true religion by protecting freedom of religion, but not to impose a religion—even the true one.[5]

Wall of separation

Williams usually argues from the point of view of the wellbeing of the church. For example, when he uses the 'wall of separation' illustration, he is expressing the fear that when the state is allowed to interfere in the church, the church will inevitably suffer.[6]

The phrase 'wall of separation' has become famous as used by Thomas Jefferson and as a commentary on the interpretation of the 'no establishment of religion' clause in the First Amendment to the United States Constitution. Williams wrote of 'the wall of separation between the garden of the church and the wilderness of the world'; Jefferson wrote of the 'wall of separation' between church and state. Williams' concern was to preserve the proper spheres of church and state and to protect the church from overweaning government; Jefferson was concentrating on preventing any establishment of religion. Timothy Hall concludes after a comparison of Williams and Thomas Jefferson, that Williams' convictions were more likely to lead to genuine religious freedom.[7] Jefferson was concerned to resist anything that to him looked like tyranny over the human mind; his goal was freedom *from* religion. Williams certainly wanted freedom from any tyranny over the conscience, but he acted from the conviction that a personal God existed and that the soul needed him. To Jefferson, the Deist, although he was tolerant and even supportive of religious services in the Capitol on Sundays, religion itself was barely relevant to society's wellbeing except to produce and support morality (a tendency also discernible in Locke).[8] This difference in outlook meant that whereas Williams would be very sensitive to the needs of consciences and beliefs other than his own, Jefferson's reasoning could be less sensitive to a violation of conscience provided the main aim of restraining religion's influence over others was achieved. Putting it another way: he was much more concerned for the non-establishment clause in the First Amendment, than for the free exercise clause, and this has persisted in recent First Amendment jurisprudence. Judicial decisions in America in the latter twentieth century have used non-establishment to exclude religious conviction from public life, and without fair reference to the original context of the First Amendment.

Williams was also concerned for the state to be given its rights as an ordinance of God. When religious tests (as in New England) are applied to public office, the state is deprived of a wealth of gifts in the unconverted world.

The city and the ship

Williams' best known images of the church and state are first the free corporation in a city which is distinct from the city and may come and go like other free corporations without affecting the city; and secondly the ship at sea in which all passengers must play their part in ensuring a safe passage but only those who wish to need attend the ship's prayers. These illustrations must not be pushed beyond their limits but they give some idea of Williams' thinking. In relation to the state, the church is one organization among others, and has no authority over others; nor does the state have any authority to demand worship of any favoured religion.[9]

Later arguments for church-state co-operation

The case for some degree of state oversight of the church has been ably argued since the seventeenth century though with more sensitivity to any possible threat of coercion. The nineteenth-century Scottish Presbyterian William Symington puts a winsome case for it in *Messiah the Prince*. His arguments for a limited state oversight of the church and support of the church are based on the obligations of the nations to obey Christ as Messiah. It is not any sort of union between church and state he will endorse, he says, not with a heathen, anti-Christian and immoral state, but only with a government 'possessing the character and subserving the purposes of the moral ordinance of God.' Moreover such states would not have authority to legislate for any internal matters of the church, but may make regulations about the church and its external interests. Such governments are, by virtue of the duty all nations are under in relation to Christ, under duty to 'recognise, favour, and support the true religion.' Ephesians 1:22, which reads, 'And he put all things under his feet and gave him as head over all things to the church,' is cited in support.[10]

The lordship of Christ over the nations is not in question, but Symington's qualifications on the kind of government with which the church may enter into union virtually excludes all governments known to man. It is dependent on the glorious days of a postmillennial eschatology which is the framework in which Symington works. Moreover, as Williams would have been quick to point out, *whose* 'true religion' is to be recognized, when even the Puritans could not agree on forms of church order and worship? Who in government is competent to decide what the true religion is? What about citizens who do not adhere to the true religion? Symington asserts that there would be no persecution or coercion, but a two-tier citizenship creates discrimination, as non-conformists historically in this country know very well.

Such systems of course, with little attention to the qualifications Symington sets out, are widely adopted in nations with some form of national religion, like the United Kingdom and Lutheran nations in Europe. Williams articulated what non-conformists have generally believed: that a church with a mere human being, let alone an unconverted monarch, as its Supreme Governor; a parish system; men who should be church elders becoming *ex officio* members of a political assembly and giving their valuable time as bishops to political matters; secular government exercising authority over the church—are all biblically unjustifiable. The constitutional arrangement in America, with 'no establishment of religion' is healthier for religion; for the church; and for the state.

The civil public square

In *The Case for Civility* Os Guinness compares three models for church and state. First, the *sacred* public square is where a preferred place in public life is given to one religion. A mild version of this is the Church of England; a strong version would be Islamic Saudi Arabia. Second, the *naked* public square is where religion is excluded, 'all religious expression inviolably private and ... the public sphere inviolably secular'– for example China, or more mildly, France. Third, Guinness argues for a *civil* public square where 'people of all faiths are equally free to enter and engage public life on the basis of their own faiths as a matter of free exercise.'[11] Roger Williams is one of Guinness' inspirations. The civil public square is something like the Rhode Island Williams fought for.

And, one may say, something like the United States of America though Guinness is concerned about dangers facing that society, 'First and most important, Americans must face the fact that the challenge of living with our deepest—that is our religiously grounded—differences is one of the world's great issues today.'[12] Respect for others is what Williams fought for and in some measure won, a government where absolute liberty of conscience was enjoyed and church and state were separated. What the west is being reminded of now is that without fundamental respect for those who differ, constitutional safeguards in themselves cannot prevent oppression of one group by another. Such respect can be inherited or learned but it endures only when it is the fruit of Christian conviction.

Chapter 14

Civility, Pluralism and Natural Law

THE THIRD QUESTION I WANT TO CONSIDER IS: CAN SOCIETY SURVIVE without a religious foundation? Typical of the thinking of the Puritan age was the expression of *A Model of Church and Civil Power* that 'Civil Peace cannot stand entire where religion is corrupted.'[1] True religion was adjudged to be essential to the stability of the state.

A moral foundation for a pluralist society

Roger Williams created in Rhode Island what we would call a pluralist society. People of all beliefs or none were welcome to settle there and worship and indeed live as they wished provided they abided by mutually agreed norms of behaviour that preserved civil peace. By the first compact in 1638 the settlers agreed to obey mutually agreed orders for the public good 'only in civil things' and the Royal Charter of 1663 provided that no-one should be 'molested ... for any differences in opinion in matters of religion,' but, 'freely ... to have their own judgements,' so long as they behaved 'peaceably and quietly, and not using this liberty to licentiousness and profaneness, nor to the civil injury or outward disturbance of others.' The problem with pluralism however is always: on what moral basis does society build? Take it one step further back: does society need a common *religious* foundation?

Roger Williams was quite content to say 'no.' There was a 'civil faithfulness, obedience, honesty, chastity, etc.,' that existed 'even amongst such as own not God nor Christ.' As biblical evidence he cited Abraham and Isaac entering into 'leagues with ungodly princes.' Against the idea that only church members should have a share in government he argued that there was a 'moral virtue, a moral fidelity, ability and honesty' which people outside the churches had 'by good nature and education, by good laws and good examples nourished and trained up in.'[2] God also commands relations of government, marriage and employment to be respected by Christians even when the 'grace of Christ' has not appeared to others in those relationships.[3] He believed that God's absolute moral law was embedded in every human being and was reflected in individual conscience and in the image of God, which had been shattered but not destroyed completely by the Fall. He was firmly within what is traditionally called the 'natural law' tradition, a school of thought that believes that God's law is written on the human heart at creation and never completely erased, and that it is adequate to ground civil society. His observations of history (other civilizations, outside Christendom) and life (particularly that of the Native Americans) satisfied him that civil government and society could exist where there was no gospel and no special (biblical) revelation.

The concept Williams was fond of using to describe the pattern of life in a pluralist society was 'civility.' In *Examiner Defended* he contrasted civil crime against the state and those of a spiritual nature against God, claiming that whereas certain sins are known to all men, men and nations have constantly differed about the true God and ways of worship; moreover, it is easier to get people to admit to the wrongness of civil crimes, whereas oppression in religious matters confirmed sinners in their beliefs.[4] Officers of justice were needed to stop 'incivilities' (crimes against the state) but different religions could exist side by side. He declared that four moral violations in particular were 'inconsistent to the converse of man with man' and were known to all people— murder, adultery, theft and lying. These did not need to be obtained from the Decalogue but were natural laws written in men's hearts. He would add the 'Golden Rule'—do as you would be done by. This becomes 'give every man his due'—a natural law principle of justice which of course entails toleration. This was offended by religious persecution.

For Williams, any government intrusion into the spiritual life was 'persecution,' namely troubling believers 'for either professing doctrine, or practising worship merely religious or spiritual' when they act according to conscience or forcing them to yield obedience to such worship or doctrine that was against their conscience.[5] The civil state on the other hand was established 'for the defence of persons, estates, families, liberties of a city or civil state, and the suppressing of uncivil or injurious persons or actions.'[6] Both conscience and government had limits. Government is limited to its responsibility to preserve peace and civility. Conscience is limited by its obligation to submit itself to the government as God's ordinance for preserving peace and civility. An example of this was his insistence that Rhode Islanders be prepared to defend their realm and pay taxes for that purpose.[7]

Other virtues, said Williams, were sociability, helpfulness, friendliness (that is, to live as neighbours), loyalty, dependability, respect for civil authority and gratitude.

The shared norms and values of 'civility' are for Williams the foundation of durable public order. It was the duty of government to allow freedom of worship for such freedom was crucial to preserving an environment where civility could flourish. Nor should even a moral code be established in detail but moral freedom should be nurtured. He believed that the Decalogue did not apply to the world except as it reflected natural law in the second table; it was for Israel, the typical nation. Governments today had to make laws and punishments as fitted their case.[8]

The failure of coercion

Williams knew that morality, no more than religious belief, could be coerced. He knew that even though 'Godliness, which is infinitely more beautiful' could be lacking in a person, there could still be moral goodness. His belief was that 'the moral capacities with which every human being is endowed are a sufficient basis for public co-operation and cohabitation.'[9] He believed that the common good of civil society depends more on the cultivation of 'civility' than on uniformity of religion. Religion's contribution indeed should be in cultivating a desire and capacity for civility— for living together in peace. The Christian religion above all provides that motivation. Christianity of course teaches virtue and morality for a higher end, but love of neighbour at least provides for peaceful cohabitation in society.

Behind Williams' struggles for peaceful co-existence was a desire to serve the 'common good' and the Christian duty to do so. In *Examiner Defended* he again uses the analogy of the ship where all must help to ensure she sails safely though none may be forced to attend common worship, and writes:

> Hence not to study, and not to endeavour the common good, and to exempt ourselves from the sense of common evil, is a treacherous baseness, a selfish monopoly, a kind of tyranny, and tendeth to the destruction both of cabin and ship, that is, of private and public safety.[10]

Did not the parable of the wheat and the tares teach something similar—good and evil reside in this world together and only the day of judgement will separate them finally?

Williams incidentally adds an argument to the weaponry of those who say 'religion causes wars.' Yes it does, he says, when it does not respect freedom of conscience and thinks that religion can be imposed. That is why the 'tenet of persecution' is bloody; that is why respecting freedom of conscience could, over the centuries, have saved 'rivers of civil blood.'[11]

Civility, good manners and the bond of society

Williams was also concerned for the manner in which debate was conducted; civility was procedural—something like our contemporary meaning of the word. He was fully aware that people differed. Living together required tolerance, not just formal toleration of different religions, but tolerance as a basic ingredient of social life. Civility in this sense provided the framework within which people could struggle for the common good. Such tolerance, said Williams, agreed most with the 'Rules of the best Politician that ever the world saw'—Jesus Christ. Williams strongly objected to the Quakers' incivility in their debate, shouting him down with constant interruptions, as well as with their well-known public displays of interrupting church services and 'prophetic' nudity.

Teresa Bejan examines the 'civility crisis' in public life today. What can provide the 'bond of society' now that the hitherto presupposed glue of true religion and Christian charity is being dissolved? How can we allow for disagreement without being disagreeable? More is needed than superficial calls for politeness if we are to avoid, on the one hand, a collapse into violent and chaotic discourse or, on the other, retreat into our own echo chambers where we refuse to hear anyone we fear will offend us or others. Bejan discusses and rejects what she calls Thomas Hobbes' 'civil silence' because it involves muting controversial subjects; she rejects too John Locke's 'civil charity.' Locke insisted on charity, a virtue that smacks of church. His 'bond of society' is trustworthiness but this led to the exclusion of atheists and Roman Catholics from equal treatment because they could not be trusted.[12] She prefers what she calls Williams' 'mere civility' because it sets the bar of the 'bond of society' lower and embraces everyone. His version of civility required less like-mindedness, more real tolerance. By 'mere civility' she means Williams' 'minimal adherence to culturally contingent rules of respectful behavior compatible with, and occasionally expressive of, contempt for others and their beliefs;' or a 'low standard, loosely applied, combined with a thick-skinned determination to tolerate what we perceive as others' incivility.'[13]

Williams' crucial contribution, concludes Bejan, was 'the insight that the commonality needed to sustain a tolerant society could be much more minimal and superficial than traditionalist defenders of religion as the *bond of society* supposed.'[14] He was under no illusion that such a society would be a peaceful, harmonious or pleasant place to live. But in a society committed to toleration of diversity and disagreement, in the 'messy real world of unmurderous coexistence between individuals divided on the fundamentals and mutually disdainful of others' contrary commitments,' 'mere civility' offers the modest hope of living with those whom one finds difficult to respect.[15] This 'unapologetically evangelical form of toleration' has 'fundamentally shaped our institutional and intellectual context' but if we are to continue to have faith in the values of toleration we must have a strong faith in the good that will come of it—a faith not unlike that which enabled Williams to tolerate his opponents. In this light, suggests Bejan intriguingly, evangelism, as a model of conversational engagement, seems uniquely well suited to characterize and sustain a commitment to ongoing, active and often heated disagreement in the public square. As Williams said, 'He that is a Briar, that is a Jew, a Turke, a Pagan, or an Anti-Christian today, may be (*when the Word of the Lord runs freely*) a member of Jesus Christ tomorrow.'[16]

Is Bejan right on Williams? Basically she is, but the further question must be asked—what enabled Williams to be so robust? Bejan, like many commentators on Williams, does not engage sufficiently with the content of his Christian belief. What enabled him to be so robust in his tolerance was his doctrine of creation. The bond of society for him was the created order; for Winthrop and the proponents of Christendom it was the gospel—and society was therefore more akin to church. For Williams, you do not oppress another in areas of belief and morals because that person is made in the image of God and is ultimately answerable to him alone. You allow freedom because the person with whom you disagree, even if truly objectionable, is free because he is made in the image of a free God. You respect people (and treat them civilly) not because of the social consequences but because of what that person is in God's sight. Moreover, humanity is fallen so needs to hear the truth—the only weapon Williams allows in the fight against idolatry. In this sense, Williams did not expect people to receive truth easily or live it out in speech or conduct so thought of it as a battle. To adopt Williams' protagonists in *The Bloudy Tenent*, Truth is of crucial importance because in spiritual things truth is absolute. Truth is, however, virtually eliminated today as a consideration in ideological discourse. Peace is more important. For Williams however truth was the priority—'having bought truth dear, we must not sell it cheap, no not for the saving of souls, though our own most precious.'[17] In the pursuit, proclamation or the preservation of truth, peace is to be maintained so far as possible but not at the expense of truth.

Given his doctrinal framework, civility as good manners is secondary to civility as peaceful co-existence. Since the Enlightenment rejected dependence on God and revelation, truth has been increasingly interpreted subjectively. In metaphysics (what is ultimately real), morals (how we should live and to what end) and epistemology (how we can be sure of anything) the answer will be based on my thoughts, desires and perceptions, not on anything objective. Today peace is also interpreted subjectively. 'You shall not disturb *the* peace' (for Williams, civility as a mode of living together) has become, 'You shall not disturb *my* peace' (civility as good manners, not being offensive). Even 'not offending' is defined subjectively—one may, of course, be offended at anything. This is political correctness. Communication must be suppressed if it offends, however true it may be, however civil the presentation. It is a form of *civil silence* but determined not by the subject matter so much as by the possible impact on the hearer. The result is an appearance of like-mindedness but it is neither deep nor real. Differences and disagreements are suppressed, not discussed. There is no need for real toleration because people are stopped from saying anything others need to tolerate. It is a far cry from what Bejan terms Roger Williams' 'cacophonous ... evangelical' view of toleration. He can 'set the bar low' because he roots his vision of peaceful co-existence in the created order, in the works and the Word of God.

Overemphasis on civility as courtesy also disadvantages those who cannot meet the social standards of civility; public debate becomes the preserve of the educated, the sophisticated, the élite. The demand for civility taken too far, becomes in effect a restriction on freedom. Williams' principle of freedom of conscience for all demands a robust willingness to be offended while speaking the truth in love.

The individual and society

Williams has been charged with being an individualist, a source of that very American trait of individualism. That is far from the truth. Williams' concept of freedom of conscience demanded civic co-operation. He fought for freedom of conscience from the impositions of both church and government but he struggled all his life to get people to work together. He knew that the success of the colony depended on the settlers' ability to distinguish between liberty and licence, to put limits on their freedom of conscience for the common good and social cohesion. Soul-liberty was never, for Williams, unbridled self-indulgence; and it certainly did not entail anarchy.

Civility as Williams saw it was the framework that allowed soul-liberty to survive in society. Like Aquinas' theory of natural law, it was a bridge that enabled Christians of differing persuasions, but also Christians with pagans, to co-exist. It was a minimal set of shared morality to enable the moral integrity of the individual to survive in harmony with the human need for social cohesion, to enable the flourishing of the individual within human society. One may argue with his precise applications; he did not deny the difficulty of establishing moral norms for a society once one has gone beyond the basics of theft, honesty, murder and adultery. Where Massachusetts overestimated the prospects of a Christian society and over-legislated accordingly, Williams opposed imposing religion or a system of morality and brought far less of a citizen's life under the web of legislation and punishment.

Miroslav Volf argues that Williams, though 'a strong religious exclusivist ... became one of the main progenitors of political pluralism.'[18] John Winthrop's exclusivism led to political exclusivism, says Volf, but Williams' to political pluralism. The reasoning behind his insistence on religious liberty was not born of indifference, nor of scepticism, nor of mere open-mindedness, but of faith. Os Guinness brings Williams to bear on the first challenge he sees as confronting Americans today, of living with one another's deepest differences, 'Truth and tough-minded debates about truth are the oxygen of a free society.'[19] That is one reason why Williams wanted people to be free in religious matters. One of the consequences of the First Amendment to the United States Constitution was, says Guinness, to shift the public discourse about religion from coercion to persuasion. The floggings, mutilations, imprisonments, banishments and executions of the seventeenth century had already given way to discussion—and Williams and Rhode Island had helped to pave the way for that. Williams would have been very much at home in a world where persuasion was the means of settling disputes. Guinness argues that today, however, 'The language of protest, pronouncement and proclamation has almost completely replaced the language of persuasion.'[20] Language has itself become an exercise of power, not of reasoned persuasion. Victory depends on making the winning statement, not recognising the truth. Where intellectual and religious freedom arise out of indifference, such power-play will be the outcome because what matters is not what is true but what works best. Where liberty is based on faith, it is because you believe that a human being will only truly find or be found by God when he is allowed to think for himself.

Is natural law enough?

The way God determined to govern the world is deeply etched into creation. For example, he made a covenant with Adam whereby Adam would govern the earth as God's vice-regent. This is reflected in a fallen world in what is perceived as a social contract or compact—a reciprocal relationship between the ruler and the ruled in human society. God's law (what he requires of us, how we are to live) is also written in our hearts. In a fallen world this is distorted and concealed but it is there, as is conscience. But can society run along these hidden, common grace lines?

The reality is of course that it has to until the gospel has worked to restore that society. Does Williams' civility work? Williams' viewpoint was that the gospel was the basis for the church but not for society. In an ideal world that is not how it would be but it is in fact exactly how most of the world operates. Christ is the king who rules both church and world, indeed rules all things for the church, but he rules them in different ways. You do not have to align God's government with human government, Christ's kingdom with the kingdoms of this world. Men and women could glean enough, he believed, from their hearts and the world around them to live together. Williams might not have said that that was the best society—though he knew that the Native Americans had many qualities, such as hospitality, modesty and kindness that had not been apparent or had got sadly lost amongst his fellow English.

Is natural law sufficient? Many will say that Williams is cheating, smuggling into his view of civility a lot of Christian thinking; that common grace is not enough to ground society; that he is operating with a concept of what some call 'middle grace,' a version of the good life that does not openly acknowledge Christian influence but is actually drawing on and is dependent on it. Williams of course was starting at another point—his goal was freedom of conscience; how society was to be run was an important consideration but secondary. He began with freedom; the Puritans began with order. They make sense from the medieval perspective; Williams makes sense from the modern perspective. Christians have no authority to impose on the world the norms of the gospel or Christian behaviour. His radical distinction between the church and the world enabled Williams to allow freedom of conscience without fear that God will be dishonoured or true religion suffer. God and the gospel, he reckoned, could fend for themselves. Remember his context. His experience of what we would call Christian society was hardly happy.

Williams reflects the current debate between what is called 'one kingdom' and 'two kingdom' theology.[21] For our present limited purposes, 'one kingdom' theology has a much higher expectation of Christ's using all of the created order including governments to bring in his kingdom; 'two kingdom' theology has much lower expectations of what Christ will accomplish through the created order in terms of his coming kingdom. Williams is very much on the 'two kingdom' side yet, unlike the way that model is sometimes portrayed, Williams was never passive or negative about civil life. He gave much of his life to it but he did not see it as significant in terms of the new creation.

Williams of course was drawing on the Bible but he read the Bible as having a 'new beginning' at the coming of Christ. He could draw on the Old Testament, and it was certainly the Word of God, but Israel was not authoritative for the church-state relationship. Freedom of worship was authorized by God and the truth is to be propagated only by Word and Spirit. Williams devoted his whole life to enabling people to be free in conscience not for its own sake, but so that they would be won by God, for the worship of God. Meanwhile civil society must rely on such resources as God gives it—and his conviction was that natural law was enough. If more was available he was not going to reject it. He simply did not anticipate that human government was one of the ways in which Christ would perfect his church or bring in his kingdom—and here he was quite at odds with most of his fellow Puritans. How 'Christian' a society might become was, in Williams' thinking, unrelated to God's work in redemption and eternity.

Williams' conviction was that Christendom needed redemption as much as the pagan Natives. He saw things with an observant and analytical eye. In the end he awaited perfection, and only Christ would bring that in.

Chapter 15

What Williams Means For Us Today

'LUTHER IS A DIFFICULT HERO,' ADMITS LYNDAL ROPER.[1] ON A SMALLER scale, that is true of Roger Williams. Perhaps all our heroes are difficult—and the better we know them the more difficult they become. Only by filtering them can we make them manageable. It would be easier to extol Williams, for example, had his exposition of Revelation not steered him into a dead end on the ministry and the church. Or if he could have held on to more continuity with the Old Testament, including the Decalogue. It would have been satisfying to report on more unequivocal evangelising among the Native Americans though he did more than many, and like others he got lost in the Apocalypse.

But he was what he was. What grasped him, grasped him deeply, profoundly—awkwardly, so far as others were concerned. The value of the individual conscience; the illegitimacy of imposing spiritually on a soul; the illegitimacy of a national or state religion; the importance of separating church and state, not merely distinguishing between them; that this is for the sake of the church, for when the wall of separation is broken down, it is the garden that suffers as the weeds from the wilderness inevitably take over; confidence that civil society can operate on the basis of natural law—at least as to its being if not its well-being; that civil government can be operated by unbelievers; patient discussion with those who disagree with us; that all this is best for the church.

His influence

Because of the significance of the issue of separation of church and state in later history, Williams is one of the most studied figures in pre-revolutionary America. Some historians have minimized his importance. Yet Rhode Island did influence others—New Jersey and Carolina, for example, were given charters with some degree of religious freedom, even while establishing the Anglican Church.[2] In 1682, Pennsylvania was established with liberty of conscience. In 1689 John Locke published his *A Letter Concerning Toleration.* John Barry quotes historians who assert that 'It is impossible to discover a single significant difference between the argument set forth by Williams and [that] later advanced by Locke;' and that 'Locke's ideas are ... simply restatements of the central arguments in favor of freedom of conscience developed by Roger Williams.'[3] W. K. Jordan concludes that Williams' argument for separation of church and state 'may be regarded as the most important contribution made during the century in this significant area of political thought.'[4] In 1689 the Toleration Act in Britain at least stopped persecution of Protestant dissent even if it fell well short of liberty in the Williams mould.

In his closing chapter Edwin Gaustad summarizes later views on, and the influence of, Williams.[5] In 1702 Cotton Mather began his discussion of Williams with an oft-quoted parable: a windmill in a Dutch town once turned so fast that it set itself and the town alight. So did the flailing sails in Williams' head disturb New England, asserted Mather. Williams proceeded to create a mess of a colony with 'Antinomians, Familists, Anabaptists, Antisabbatarians, Arminians, Socinians, Quakers, Ranters—everything in the world but Roman Catholics and real Christians.'[6] By an eighteenth-century Rhode Island Baptist, John Callender, Williams was called, 'one of the most disinterested men that ever lived, a most pious and heavenly minded soul.' Stephen Hopkins, a Quaker, and many times a governor of the colony between 1755 and 1768, honoured Williams for being the 'first legislator in the world ... that fully and effectively provided for and established a free, full, and absolute liberty of conscience.' The first major history to rehabilitate Williams was the Baptist Isaac Backus' *A History of New England with Particular Reference to the Denomination of Christians called Baptists*. Baptists flourished in the era of religious freedom after the Revolution and fought widely for separation of church and state. Madison and Jefferson may have known of Williams though their arguments for separation were phrased in secular terms. Certainly no direct connection with Williams can be traced. 'I have sworn upon the altar of god eternal hostility against every form of tyranny over the mind of man,' Jefferson wrote. Williams would have heartily agreed, though he might not have sworn, and his God would have been a lot greater than whatever Jefferson worshipped.

Varied conclusions

'A polemical porcupine' was how John Quincy Adams described Williams. In the twentieth century, Williams was lauded as a political liberal and democrat. Perry Miller restored the Puritans to credibility and restored too his religion to Williams—though Miller seemed to think Williams was the only Puritan to use typology. In 1962 Williams appeared in a footnote to a Supreme Court decision that state-mandated prayer violated the First

Amendment. Supreme Court battles on this Amendment have been frequent and fierce in recent years.

Other views on Williams have appeared in recent years. In 2008 Martha Nussbaum drew heavily on him to protect the American tradition of religious equality which she sees as under threat from government and courts.[7] She does so eloquently, but at the expense of distortion. The Williams she portrays is a secularized shadow of the seventeenth century Puritan agitator.

Timothy Hall in *Separating Church and State* concludes:

> The price Williams paid for freedom of conscience was the de-Christianization of Christian America. To him, at least, this was not an exorbitant price, because he believed that Christian America had never existed and never would. He cared too deeply about God and the church to trivialize them with public professions of religiousness. Nevertheless, because his contemporaries could not accept that price, they labeled Williams a fanatic and forgot about him. He has few knowledgeable supporters in the present day for the same reason. He alienates Jeffersonians by the fervency of his faith and believers by the secularism of his political vision.[8]

John Barry considers that 'Williams' ideas became quintessentially American.' He adds however:

> So did John Winthrop's. Williams saw the individual standing alone with God ... Winthrop saw a state committed to Christian ideals, demanding conformity and imposing community standards upon individuals. Between Williams's views on one side and those of Winthrop on the other was a tension, and that very tension was also quintessentially American. It was in that tension that the American soul was being created.[9]

Williams and the contemporary context

We too live in 'wonderful searching, disputing, and dissenting times.'[10] If Williams can only help us be aware of the possibilities of the days in which we live instead of the downbeat sense of loss that Christians feel, he will have done something for us.

He reminds us how to live together. His profound respect for human beings as creatures of God and answerable to him first and last, is the foundation of civil society. As Teresa Bejan says, he helps us by setting the bar for co-existence lower.

He teaches Christians that though their world view may be true, it is not to be forced on others, neither does being a Christian entail a divine right to rule. We are all prone to making mistakes when seeking to apply biblical beliefs in the public square.

He teaches us to analyse and to question. No doubt what we call a Christian culture is a good thing. We would rather live in a culture profoundly influenced by the gospel (as would many who have no affection for Christianity) than not. Williams teaches us, however, to be more critical without being cynical about just how Christian the west's culture has been. Under hostile pressure, Christians are inclined to look at the past through rose-tinted glasses. Much of what we think of as 'Christian' in our history does not always bear close biblical scrutiny. Our evangelical forefathers were nothing like as sanguine about their 'Christian' society as we are.

The tearing away of much that we have assumed to be unassailable is making us think again about what exactly is Christian and what is cultural accretion. We have been made to think, for example, about discrimination against and insensitivity to minorities; about expressions of religion in public life; about the co-existence of different religions and moral codes; about how the church should relate to an increasingly unsympathetic state. Secular liberal culture is to a large extent a Christian culture which has lost its spiritual dynamism but are Christians clear about what is Christian and what is merely liberal? The American Right is accused of baptizing the flag, the constitution and capitalism. British evangelicals are sometimes in danger of doing the same with British Protestant history and Western, 'Christian' culture more generally. Yet it is always dangerous for the church to identify itself, and be identified, with any single cultural manifestation of gospel influence, however deep and rich.

Williams reminds us, too, where the influence of the gospel in society ultimately comes from. It is neither through government action nor the established church. Spiritual life, power and change have come through great spiritual movements and revivals that have profoundly affected substantial sections of the population.

He reminds us that while in a minority (which is the position most Christians in history have found themselves) Christians can live Christianly without Christendom. 'Render to Caesar the things that are Caesar's, and to God the things that are God's' (Matthew 22:21) and the coming of the kingdom that is not of this world (John 18:36) do not require a Christian culture even if such a society is the best place to live. We will do what good we can in politics and society, including fighting for the benefits of a Christian worldview and ethics, but Christians should primarily be working for the coming of Christ's kingdom, not focusing on preserving or retrieving a so-called Christian culture. Preaching the gospel is the church's task, the Great Commission. The Word will change cultures as well as save souls. Individual Christians of course should follow whatever vocation the Lord has for them in public life—serving the public, as Williams would have said.

He reminds us too that no man or institution should exercise authority over another unless God ordains it. Williams realized of course that individuals and the church could not live in a vacuum unrelated to the state; but under God the conscience should be free; the church should be free; the state should be free. So, under God, they will be best placed to prosper. These are the convictions for which Roger Williams lived and for which he should be remembered.

Roger Williams and the Conversion of Native Americans

THE FIRST KNOWN REFERENCE BY WILLIAMS TO THE CONVERSION OF Native Americans is in a letter to John Winthrop in 1632, disclaiming any desire to be an elder in a church, 'if the Lord please to grant my desires, that I may intend what I long after, the natives' souls.'[1] During the Pequot War (1636–38) he blamed the war on the English lack of 'sense (I speak for the general that I can hear of) of their souls' condition.'[2] In February 1637 he was still optimistic in writing to Winthrop:

> Sir I hope shortly to send you good news of great hopes the Lord hath sprung up in mine eye of many a poor Indian soul enquiring after God. I have convinced hundreds at home and abroad that in point of Religion they are all wandering etc. ... I hope the time is not long that some shall truly bless the God of Heaven that ever they saw the face of English men.[3]

In *A Key* he wrote in 1643 of his hope that the book would help those who may have opportunity to speak with:

> Some of these their wild brethren and Sisters ... a word for their and our glorious Maker, which may also prove some preparatory mercy to their Soules ... which who knows (in God's holy season) may rise to the exalting of the Lord Jesus Christ in their conversion, and salvation.[4]

In 1643, just before Williams' *A Key*, *New Englands First Fruits* was published in London by New Englanders to show that New England was indeed engaged in mission to the Natives. It recounted the conversion of a Pequot called Wequash. The report in *The Great Works of Christ in America* begins by describing how in the days leading to the Pequot War in 1637 the 'Ammonites' (i.e. the Native Americans) had made themselves stink before the New English 'Israel.'[5] Wequash had been a captain of the Pequots but 'revolted' from them. After five or six hundred Pequots 'were dismissed from a world that was burdened with them' in the fire at the fort, Wequash was so amazed at the power of 'the Englishman's God' that he 'went about the colony of Connecticut with bitter lamentations "that he did not know Jesus Christ", until the good people there instructed him.' At last the Natives poisoned him for his religion. Thomas Shepard of Cambridge, Massachusetts, exulted that Wequash:

> Is dead, and certainly in heaven: gloriously did the grace of Christ shine forth in his conversation, a year and half before his death; he knew Christ, he loved Christ, he preached Christ up and down; and then suffered martyrdom for Christ.[6]

In *A Key* Williams gave his version of events. He wrote that he had 'many solemn discourses' with all sorts of nations among the Natives:

I know there is no small preparation in the hearts of multitudes of them. I know their many solemn confessions to myself, and one to another of their lost wandering conditions. I know strong convictions upon the consciences of many of them, and their desires uttered that way. I know not with how little knowledge and grace of Christ the Lord may save, and therefore neither will despair, nor report much.[7]

He proceeds to recount that two days before Wequash died he was told that 'my old friend' Wequash lay very sick and Williams wanted to see him. He 'closed with' Wequash concerning his soul. Wequash told Williams that some two or three years before he had lodged at his house, Williams had acquainted him with the condition of all mankind, and his own in particular, how God created man and all things, how man fell from God, of his present enmity against God, and the wrath of God against him until repentance; that

Williams' words were never out of his heart to this day, and that he 'much pray to Jesus Christ.' I told him, said Williams, that 'so did many English, French and Dutch, who had never turned to God, nor loved him.' He replied in broken English, 'Me so big naughty heart, me heart all one stone!' Williams says that this was the 'summe of our last parting until our general meeting [presumably Williams means after death].'[8]

Williams goes on to say that all are enquiring 'what have the English done in those parts towards the converting of the Indians?' He was 'comfortably persuaded' that the Father of Spirits would in due season persuade these:

Gentiles of America to partake of the mercies of Europe, and then shall be fulfilled what is written by the prophet Malachi, from the rising of the Sunne (in Europe) to the going down of the same (in

America) my Name shall be great among the Gentiles. So I desire to
hope and pray.[9]

John Cotton was less hopeful.

> Though a form of Christian religion may be professed amongst
> Christians with some facility: yet it is not so easy a matter to gain
> these pagan Indians so much as to a form of our Religion, and
> to hold it, howsoever Mr Williams did promise himself greater
> possibilities.[10]

In 1645 in *Christenings Make Not Christians* Williams claimed
that he could have made 'many thousands' of the Natives turn
to Christianity, but that such conversions would have been
'antichristian,' comparable to the false conversions of the Jesuits.
They would not be conversions to God, but 'subversion of the souls
of millions in Christendom.'[11] He criticized the superficial views
of those who boasted that they had caused Native Americans
to obey the Ten Commandments, when Williams saw those
same Natives openly still practising their public pagan 'worship
of devils.'[12] For this reason Williams was loath to impose the
Lord's Day on them—they first need to turn to God or their
hearts are not capable of worship on any day.[13] The Natives like
everyone else needed new birth, not external conversion to a
false form of worship; perhaps he believed they also needed the
pure model of true primitive worship, which he believed would
only be introduced when the Lord raised up new apostles. The
same convictions about the absence of apostolic authority in
ministry would have prevented Williams from ever believing that
he or anyone else had divine authority to preach to the Native
Americans, and that most conversions achieved by this method
would be false.

In *Yet More Bloudy* he agrees with John Cotton, in that until the
plagues of Revelation 15 were completed, and Antichrist brought

down, and apostles raised up, little in the way of conversion of the nations could be expected but 'in the mean [time] I commend the pious Endeavours of any (professing ministry or not) to do good to the souls of all men as we have opportunity.'[14] He asserts the difficulty of gaining enough proficiency in the language to be able to communicate 'matters of heaven' and through his character mouthpiece Truth he relates an incident in Thomas Shepard's account of John Eliot's ministry, where an old Native American, being offered a new coat by Eliot, had to ask what the preacher said. Peace, the opposing character, then replies that if he could not be made to understand the offer of a coat, he would hardly be able to understand the offer of the garment of the righteousness of Christ. Truth responds, 'Neither you (sweet Peace) nor I express this much to damp Mr Eliot or any from doing all the good they can, while opportunity lasts in any true Christian way, but to shew how great that mistake is, that pretends such a true preaching of Christ Jesus to them in their own language.'[15]

His interpretation of Revelation, the absence of purity and apostolic authority in the church, the lack of authority in the ministry, and also the fear of anything approaching coercion, would have combined to hold Williams back in his missionary efforts. In *George Fox Digg'd out of his Burrowes*, in a section asserting the divine origin of Scripture, he wrote:

> When we deal with the Indians about Religion, our work is to prove unto them by Reason, (i) that the Bible is God's Word, for by Nature they are much affected with a kind of Deity to be in Writing: (ii) that all their Revelations, and Visions, and Dreams (in which the Devil wonderfully abuseth them) are False and Cheating; (iii) that this Scripture or Writing we pretend to is from God, [which they must know] by their own experience, because it agrees with their own Consciences, reproving them for those sins their Souls say they are guilty of.[16]

Williams thus, towards the end of his life, argues for what we might call today an apologetic model, focusing on the understanding, ensuring the potential convert clearly understood what he was doing. Cotton in 1648 had criticised him, and we can understand why, for not taking the opportunity he had to preach to the Natives to bring about true conversions; but Cotton saw too that Williams' theology, what Cotton called his 'corrupt principles,' prevented him believing that any true church or apostles could come on the earth 'till Antichrist be abolished out of the world.'[17]

Williams' fear of coerced conversions is reflected in a letter of 1654, shortly after his return from his second visit to London, written to the Court of Massachusetts, imploring it to refrain from war with the Narragansett and other Natives. Williams relates that just before leaving for England (in 1652) he had been presented with a petition by the sachems for the 'high sachems' of England that they might not be forced from their religion, or have war waged on them for not changing their religion. They claimed they were daily visited with threats by 'Indians from Massachusetts' that 'if they would not pray they should be destroyed by war.' Williams reminds the members of the Court that they too were once persecuted and 'hath not the God of peace and the Father of Mercies made these Natives more friendly in this Wilderness than our Native Countrymen in our own land to us?' Williams pointedly resists, he says, the temptation to trouble the Court with considering whether he has been 'a friend to the Natives turning to Civility and Christianity,' but he would ask Massachusetts to consider the inconsistency between two objects, 'the Glorious Conversion of the Indians in New England, and the Unnecessary Wars and cruel Destruction of the Indians in New England.'[18]

After this letter of 1654, and the passing reference in *George Fox* in 1676, there is little mention of Native American conversions until *A Brief Reply* to John Eliot. There is one page in which Williams deals with the conversion of Native Americans. John Eliot of course had known considerable success since 1646 in preaching to the Native Americans, founding fourteen towns of 'praying Indians,' about 150 such converts living in each town. However, these towns had been decimated in King Philip's War in 1675–76 although Eliot (who outlived Williams by seven years) had re-established four towns. Williams' devastating critique was that:

> They might speak or do something as they are taught and this conversion of the Indians appears as the French and Spanish conversions. But if their leaders be prepared in error, how can their duties be considered true or according to the Gospel? As for those whom Eliot calls true converts, we must wonder of the wisdom of their conversion.[19]

Williams is at the very least clearly sceptical about the Native American conversions and appears to criticize Eliot's dealings with the sachems.

There were certainly serious misgivings among the New England colonists about the conversions among Native Americans. King Philip's War was due to many things, including increasing encroachment on forestland and loss of native political autonomy and cultural independence. Some alleged that the fear of forced conversion was among the reasons for the war. The Christian 'praying Indians' took different sides—some worked with the English as spies and guides, some tried to stay neutral, others fought against the English. The War deepened divisions and heightened suspicions between the races. For Williams it seems to have intensified his already deep-rooted caution about attempts to convert the Native Americans.

One possible change in Williams was his willingness, by 1654, to consider that 'Civility may be a leading step to Christianity.'[20] Earlier, for example in *A Key*, he had seen more of the positive sides of Native American culture and did not suggest they needed to be moved from 'barbarism to civility' as a step to true conversion, even though preaching of the gospel would lead to 'civility.' In 1654 he wrote that 'All Indians are Extremely treacherous,' and in 1668 he wrote to Massachusetts 'I abhor most of their Customs. I know they are Barbarous,' which strikes a somewhat different note from the predominant tone of *A Key*, though Williams was never uncritical of the Native Americans.[21]

The relationship with John Eliot was doubtless coloured by the fact that Eliot had been one of the ministers who with Hooker, Cotton and others took Williams to task for his views in the early years in Boston and then exiled him. Eliot also wrote in justification of the Court's decision and was further involved in the banishment of Anne Hutchinson, with whom Williams did not agree although he believed she had been unfairly treated.[22] Eliot's endeavours and success with the Native Americans after 1646 was widely publicized in England: in pleading with Massachusetts to avoid war in 1654 Williams argued that God's honour was at stake:

> How greatly the name of God is concerned in this Affaire; for it Can not be hid, how all England and other nations ring with the glorious Conversion of the Indians of New England. You know how many books are dispersed throughout the nation of the subject (in some of them the Nariganset Chiefe Sachims are publicly branded for refusing to pray and be converted).[23]

Studies even at the time and later have indicated that Native Americans were resistant to Christianity, particularly the Narragansetts; in 1674 Eliot's colleague Daniel Gookin blamed the bad example of the English in Rhode Island. In Thomas Shepard's book referred to above, an incident is recounted from Eliot, that he had asked a Native American chief why they had not learned the gospel from Mr Williams 'who had lived among them divers years?' The sachem replied that he did not care to learn from him 'because he is no good man but goes out and works on the Sabbath day.'[24] It was not until the First Great Awakening of the 1730s and 1740s that significant numbers of Narragansetts professed Christian faith.

The discovery of *A Brief Reply* shows an essential continuity, despite modifications, in Williams' thinking. He continued to be sceptical of anything he regarded as heavy-handed methods of proselytisation and preferred his long-term friendship with occasional sermons to Native Americans over large-scale evangelisation.

Bibliography

Works by Roger Williams

A Key into the Language of America (1643)

Mr. Cottons letter lately printed, examined and answered (1644)

Queries of Highest Consideration (1644)

The Bloudy Tenent of Persecution for Cause of Conscience (1644)

Christenings Make Not Christians (1645)

The Bloudy Tenent Yet More Bloudy (1652)

Experiments of Spiritual Life and Health (1652)

The Fourth Paper Presented by Major Butler (1652)

The Hireling Ministry None of Christ's (1652)

The Examiner—Defended in a Fair and Sober Answer (1652)

George Fox Digg'd out of His Burrowes (1676)

These works are contained in *The Complete Writings of Roger Williams* in seven volumes published by Russell & Russell, New York, 1963, reprinted 2005 by the Baptist Standard Bearer, Inc. This collection also contains the *Letter of Mr. John Cotton* (1643) and

John Cotton's Answer to Roger Williams (1647). Volume 6 is a selection of Williams' letters.

Secondary and critical works on Roger Williams

Barry, John M., *Roger Williams and the Creation of the American Soul* (Viking, 2012)

Brockunier, Samuel H., *The Irrepressible Democrat* (The Ronald Press Company, 1940)

Byrd Jr., James P., *The Challenges of Roger Williams* (Mercer University Press, 2002)

Camp, L. Raymond, *Roger Williams, God's Apostle of Advocacy* (Edwin Mellen Press, 1989)

Davis, James Calvin, *The Moral Theology of Roger Williams* (Westminster John Knox Press, 2004)

Ernst, James E., *The Political Thought of Roger Williams* (University of Washington Press, 1929)

Fisher, L.D., J.S. Lemons and L. Mason-Brown, *Decoding Roger Williams* (Baylor University Press, 2014)

Gaustad, Edwin S., *Liberty of Conscience* (Judson Press, 1999)

——., *Roger Williams—Lives and Legacies* (Oxford University Press, 2005)

Gilpin, W. Clark, *The Millenarian Piety of Roger Williams* (University of Chicago Press, 1979)

Hall, Timothy L., *Separating Church and State: Roger Williams and Religious Liberty* (University of Illinois Press, 1998)

Knowles, James D., *Memoir of Roger Williams, the Founder of the State of Rhode Island* (BiblioLife; first published: Lincoln, Edmands and Co., Boston, 1834)

LaFantasie, Glenn W., *The Correspondence of Roger Williams, Volumes 1 and 2* (Rhode Island Historical Society, 1988)

Miller, Perry, *Roger Williams: His Contribution to the American Tradition* (Atheneum, New York, 1962)

Morgan, Edmund S., *Roger Williams, The Church and the State* (W.W. Norton, 2006)

Polishook, Irwin H., *Roger Williams, John Cotton and Religious Freedom* (Prentice-Hall, Inc., New Jersey, 1967)

Spurgin, Hugh, *Roger Williams and Puritan Radicalism in the English Separatist Tradition* (Edwin Mellen Press, 1989)

Winslow, Ola, *Master Roger Williams* (Macmillan, 1957)

Other critical works

Adair, John, *Puritans* (Sutton Publishing, 1998)

Bejan, Teresa M., *Mere Civility: Disagreement and the Limits of Toleration* (Harvard University Press, 2017)

Bremer, Francis J., *The Puritan Experiment* (University Press of New England, 1995)

Coffey, John, *Persecution and Toleration in Protestant England 1558–1689* (Longman, 2000)

——, *Politics, Religion and the British Revolutions: The Mind of Samuel Rutherford* (Cambridge University Press, 1997)

Coffey, John, and Paul C.H. Lim, *The Cambridge Companion to Puritanism* (Cambridge University Press, 2008)

D'Costa, Gavin, Tariq Modood and Julian Rivers, *Religion in a Liberal State* (Cambridge University Press, 2013)

Emerson, Everett, *John Cotton* (Twayne Publishers, 1965)

Gribben, Crawford, *The Puritan Millennium: Literature and Theology 1550–1682* (Paternoster, 2008)

Guinness, Os, *The Case for Civility* (HarperOne, 2008)

——., *The Global Public Square* (IVP, 2013)

Helwys, Thomas, *A Short Declaration of the Mystery of Iniquity* (Mercer University Press, 1998)

Hill, Christopher, *Antichrist in Seventeenth-Century England* (Oxford University Press, 1971)

Lamont, W.M., *Godly Rule: Politics and Religion 1603–60* (Macmillan, 1969)

Locke, J., *A Letter Concerning Toleration* (Digireads.com, 2005)

Maclure, J., and Charles Taylor, *Secularism and Freedom of Conscience* (Harvard University Press, 2011)

Mather, Cotton, *The Great Works of Christ in America, Volumes 1 and 2* (Banner of Truth, 1979)

Morgan, Edmund, *The Puritan Dilemma: The Story of John Winthrop* (Longman, 1999)

Murray, Iain, *The Puritan Hope* (Banner of Truth, 1971)

Nussbaum, Martha, *Liberty of Conscience: In Defense of America's Tradition of Religious Equality* (Basic Books, 2008)

Rutherford, Samuel, *Conscience, Liberty and God's Word* (Gospel Covenant Publications, 2011). This is a modern edition of *A Free Disputation Against Pretended Liberty of Conscience* (London, 1649)

——., *Lex, Rex, or The Law and the Prince* (Robert Ogle and Oliver & Boyd, 1843)

Symington, William, *Messiah the Prince, or the Mediatorial Dominion of Jesus Christ* (BiblioLife, 2009)

Van Til, L. John, *Liberty of Conscience: The History of a Puritan Idea* (P&R Publishing, 1972)

Volf, Miroslav, *Flourishing: Why we need Religion in a Globalized World* (Yale University Press, 2015)

Endnotes

Introduction

1. Letter dated September 1657 from Rhode Island to United Colonies Commissioners, in *Collections of Rhode Island Historical Society*, Vol. 5 (Providence, 1843), p. 120.

2. John Barry, *Roger Williams and the Creation of the American Soul* (Viking, 2012), p. 389.

3. See a letter from Williams to the then Governor of Massachusetts, Major John Endecott, in 1651 titled, 'Upon occasion of the late persecution of Mr Clarke and Obadiah Homes', *The Complete Writings of Roger Williams*, Vol. 4 (Baptist Standard Bearer, Inc., 2005), p. 518. Future references to this edition will be given as *Complete Writings* followed by the volume and page number. Note that volume 1 has two paginations. References are to the page numbers nearest the spine.

4. Teresa Bejan, *Mere Civility: Disagreement and the Limits of Toleration* (Harvard University Press, 2017), p. 12.

Chapter 1: Early Life

1. Article LXXXVI of 'The Confession of Faith of John Smyth and his People in 102 Articles; the original of which was found in 1871 in York Minster' (translated from a copy in the Archives of the Amsterdam Mennonite Church, 16 pages folio, No. 1365 as Appendix II in Jakob Gijsbert de Hoop Scheffer, History of the Free churchmen called the Brownists, Pilgrim fathers and Baptists in the Dutch republic, 1581–1701 (Ithaca, NY: Andrus & Church, 1922).

2. The label 'General' indicated that these Baptists believed that Christ's death was for all—a 'general' atonement; 'Particular' derived from the Calvinistic belief that Christ, by his death, intended to save only a 'particular' people.

3. For Williams' correspondence with Anne Sadleir, see Glenn W. LaFantasie, *The Correspondence of Roger Williams*, Vol. 1 (Rhode Island Historical Society, 1988), pp. 356–66. Future references to this edition will be given as *Correspondence* followed by the volume and page number.

Chapter 2: Student, Chaplain, Pilgrim

1. Samuel Brockunier, *The Irrepressible Democrat* (The Ronald Press Company, 1940), p. 18.

2. *Correspondence*, Vol. 1, p. 11, note 7.

3. *Complete Writings*, Vol. 5, 'To the People called Quakers,' unnumbered page.

4. *Correspondence*, Vol. 2, p. 630.

5. 'Eikonoclastes, In Answer to a book entitled Eikon Basilike', *A Complete Collection of Historical, Political and Miscellaneous Works of John Milton*, Vol. 1 (A. Millar, 1738), p. 423.

6. Ola Winslow, *Master Roger Williams* (Macmillan, 1957), pp. 77–8.

7. *Correspondence*, Vol. 1, pp. 4–7.

8. *Correspondence*, Vol. 1, p. 2.

9. *Complete Writings*, Vol. 4, p. 65.

10. *Complete Writings*, Vol. 1, p. 358.

Chapter 3: New England

1. Francis J. Bremer, *The Puritan Experiment* (University Press of New England, 1995), p. 87.

2. John Milton, *Areopagitica and Other Writings* (Penguin, 2014), p. 132.

Chapter 4: Godly Minister or Troubler of Israel?

1. Barry, *Roger Williams and the Creation of the American Soul*, p. 128.

2. *Correspondence*, Vol. 2, p. 630.

3. Edmund Morgan, *The Puritan Dilemma: The Story of John Winthrop* (Longman, 1999), p. 103.

4. *Correspondence*, Vol. 1, p. 8.

5. The full title was, *A Key into the Language of America: or, An help to the Language of the*

Natives in that part of America called New England. Together with brief observations of the Customs, Manners and Worships, etc. of the Aforesaid Natives, in Peace and War, in Life and Death ....

6. *Complete Writings*, Vol. 1, p. 99.

7. Cited in Barry, *Roger Williams and the Creation of the American Soul*, p. 167.

8. *Complete Writings*, Vol. 1, p. 22–23

9. W. Clark Gilpin, *The Millenarian Piety of Roger Williams* (University of Chicago Press, 1979) p. 45.

10. *Complete Writings*, Vol. 2, p. 41.

11. *Complete Writings*, Vol. 1, p. 379.

12. *Complete Writings*, Vol. 2, p. 14.

13. *Complete Writings*, Vol. 2, p. 50.

Chapter 5: The New England Way

1. Bremer, *The Puritan Experiment*, p. 87.

2. Morgan, *The Puritan Dilemma*, p. 80.

3. In England the number of capital crimes amounted to over fifty in the seventeenth century and rose to 160 by the time of William Blackstone's *Commentaries* in the mid-eighteenth century. See *Complete Writings*, Vol. 4, p. 287.

4. Bremer, *The Puritan Experiment*, p. 106.

5. *Complete Writings*, Vol. 4, p. 389.

Chapter 6: Rhode Island

1. *Correspondence*, Vol. 2, p. 610.

2. *Correspondence*, Vol. 2, pp. 610–11.

3. *Complete Writings*, Vol. 1, p. 163.

4. *Correspondence*, Vol. 2, p. 609.

5. *Correspondence*, Vol. 2, p. 750.

6. *Complete Writings*, Vol. 2, p. 18.

7. *Complete Writings*, Vol. 2, p. 751.

8. *Correspondence*, Vol. 2, p. 750.

9. *Correspondence*, Vol. 2, p. 611.

10. *Correspondence*, Vol. 2, p. 750.

11. *Correspondence*, Vol. 2, p. 485.

12. *Correspondence*, Vol. 2, p. 751.

13. Stipulated in a deed of 1661. See Barry, *Williams and the Creation of the American Soul*, p. 220.

14. Winslow, *Master Roger Williams*, p. 137.

15. John Winthrop, *The History of New England from 1630–1649*, Vol. 1 (Massachusetts Historical Society, 1825), p. 283.

16. James D. Knowles, *Memoir of Roger Williams, the Founder of the State of Rhode Island* (BiblioLife, 2009), p. 111.

17. *Correspondence*, Vol. 1, p. 54.

18. Edwin Gaustad, *Liberty of Conscience* (Judson Press, 1999), p. 38.

19. Barry, *Roger Williams and the Creation of the American Soul*, p. 225.

20. Brockunier, *The Irrepressible Democrat*, p. 127.

21. Gaustad, *Liberty of Conscience*, pp. 52–3.

22. Cotton Mather, *Great Works of Christ in America*, Vol. 2 (Banner of Truth, 1979), p. 519.

23. Mather, *Great Works of Christ in America*, Vol. 2, p. 499.

24. *Correspondence*, Vol. 2, p. 611.

25. *Correspondence*, Vol. 1, p. 89. See also Barry, *Roger Williams and the Creation of the American Soul*, p. 241.

26. *Correspondence*, Vol. 2, p. 102.

Chapter 7: Church in Rhode Island?

1. A 'sacred' public square is where a religion is dominant; a 'naked' public square is where religion is absent or banned from public display or obvious influence.

2. Gilpin, *The Millenarian Piety of Roger Williams*, p. 54.

3. James P. Byrd Jr. tabulates Bible references in Roger Williams' writings and counts the highest number, 306, from the book of Revelation; the next is Matthew with 214. See James P. Byrd Jr., 'Appendix', *The Challenges of Roger Williams* (Mercer University Press, 2002).

4. *Complete Writings*, Vol. 7, p. 158.

5. *Complete Writings*, Vol. 7, p. 160.

6. *Complete Writings*, Vol. 7, p. 159.

7. Gilpin, *The Millenarian Piety of Roger Williams*, p. 95.

8. John Owen, 'Nature and Causes of Apostasy from the Gospel', *The Works of John Owen*, Vol. 7 (Banner of Truth, 1965), p. 71.
9. Knowles, *Memoir of Roger Williams*, pp. 173, 177.
10. *Correspondence*, Vol. 2, pp. 778–79, note 4.
11. *Correspondence*, Vol. 2, p. 617.
12. Cited in L.D. Fisher, J.S. Lemons and L. Mason-Brown, *Decoding Roger Williams* (Baylor University Press, 2014), p. 42.
13. Winton U. Solberg, *Redeem the Time: The Puritan Sabbath in Early America* (Harvard University Press, 1977), pp. 194–95.

Chapter 8: A Charter

1. Brockunier, *The Irrepressible Democrat*, p. 129.
2. Gaustad, *Liberty of Conscience*, p. 55.
3. *Correspondence*, Vol. 1, p. 215.
4. Cited in Brockunier, *The Irrepressible Democrat*, p. 146.
5. A member of the Narragansett tribe told the present author in 2016 that the book is still of use in teaching the language.
6. *Complete Writings*, Vol. 1, p. 80.
7. *Complete Writings*, Vol. 1, p. 152.
8. *Complete Writings*, Vol. 1, p. 81, note 15. See the Appendix for a fuller discussion of Williams' views on conversion of Native Americans.
9. *Complete Writings*, Vol. 4, pp. 370–71.
10. *Complete Writings*, Vol. 1, p. 392.
11. *Complete Writings*, Vol. 4, p. 227.
12. Brockunier, *The Irrepressible Democrat*, p. 245.

Chapter 9: The Bloudy Tenent

1. *Complete Writings*, Vol. 3, p. 9.
2. *Complete Writings*, Vol. 3, p. 41.
3. *Complete Writings*, Vol. 3, p. 63.
4. *Complete Writings*, Vol. 3, p. 66.
5. *Complete Writings*, Vol. 3, p. 118.
6. *Complete Writings*, Vol. 3, p. 125.
7. *Complete Writings*, Vol. 3, p. 198.

8. *Complete Writings*, Vol. 3, p. 144.

9. Cited in Roger Williams, *The Bloudy Tenent* (BiblioLife, 2010), p. 117.

10. Cited in Williams, *The Bloudy Tenent*, p. 167.

11. *Complete Writings*, Vol. 3, p. 173.

12. *Complete Writings*, Vol. 3, p. 200.

13. *Complete Writings*, Vol. 3, p. 205.

14. *Complete Writings*, Vol. 3, p. 238.

15. *Complete Writings*, Vol. 3, p. 249.

16. *Complete Writings*, Vol. 3, p. 343.

17. Samuel Rutherford, 'Question IV', *Lex, Rex, or The Law and the Prince* (Robert Ogle and Oliver & Boyd, 1843).

18. William Symington, *Messiah the Prince, or the Mediatorial Dominion of Jesus Christ* (BiblioLife, 2009), p. 213.

19. *Complete Writings*, Vol. 3, p. 250.

20. *Complete Writings*, Vol. 3, p. 249.

21. *Complete Writings*, Vol. 3, p. 416.

22. *Complete Writings*, Vol. 3, pp. 293–96.

23. *Complete Writings*, Vol. 3, pp. 372–73.

24. *Complete Writings*, Vol. 3, pp. 399–400.

25. *Complete Writings*, Vol. 3, p. 189.

26. *Complete Writings*, Vol. 3, p. 72.

27. *Complete Writings*, Vol. 3, pp. 73–4.

28. Gaustad, *Liberty of Conscience*, p. 70.

Chapter 10: Trying to Make it Work

1. *Complete Writings*, Vol. 1, p. 312.

2. *Complete Writings*, Vol. 1, p. 381.

3. *Complete Writings*, Vol. 1, p. 392.

4. *Complete Writings*, Vol. 2, p. 19.

5. Barry, *Roger Williams and the Creation of the American Soul*, p. 340.

6. Barry, *Roger Williams and the Creation of the American Soul*, p. 352.

7. Cited in Irwin H. Polishook, *Roger Williams, John Cotton and Religious Freedom* (Prentice Hall, 1967), p. 112.

8. Polishook, *Roger Williams, John Cotton and Religious Freedom*, p. 113.

9.   Polishook, *Roger Williams, John Cotton and Religious Freedom*, p. 116.

10. Peter Ackroyd, *The History of England Volume III: Civil War* (Macmillan, 2014), p. 323.

11. *Correspondence*, Vol. 1, pp. 373–79.

12. In the background too was a reaction to the publication in 1652 of the Racovian Catechism, promoting the heresy of Socinianism (early Unitarianism).

13. *Complete Writings*, Vol. 4, p. 383.

14. *Complete Writings*, Vol. 7, p. 169.

15. Gaustad, *Liberty of Conscience*, p. 103.

16. *Complete Writings*, Vol. 4, p. 7.

17. *Complete Writings*, Vol. 4, pp. 347–48.

18. *Complete Writings*, Vol. 4, p. 414.

19. *Complete Writings*, Vol. 4, p. 493.

20. Everett Emerson, *John Cotton* (Twayne Publishers, 1965), p. 140.

Chapter 11: Last Battles

1.   *Correspondence*, Vol. 2, p. 784.

2.   *Correspondence*, Vol. 2, pp. 397–98.

3.   *Correspondence*, Vol. 2, pp. 423–24.

4.   Brockunier, *The Irrepressible Democrat*, p. 255.

5.   Barry, *Roger Williams and the Creation of the American Soul*, pp. 389, 310.

6.   *Correspondence*, Vol. 2, p. 615.

7.   *Correspondence*, Vol. 2, p. 263.

8.   Gaustad, *Liberty of Conscience*, p. 163.

9.   *Correspondence*, Vol. 2, p. 695.

10. Brockunier, *The Irrepressible Democrat*, pp. 243, 245, 255.

11. Bejan, *Mere Civility*, p. 76.

12. *Correspondence*, Vol. 1, p. 333.

13. *Correspondence*, Vol. 2, p. 699.

14. *Correspondence*, Vol. 2, pp. 778–79, note 4.

15. *Correspondence*, Vol. 2, pp. 777–80.

16. *Correspondence*, Vol. 2, pp. 777–80.

17. Cited in Leighton H. James, 'Roger Williams: The earliest legislator for a full and

absolute liberty of conscience,' *1976 Westminster Conference Papers: The Puritan Experiment in the New World* (Tentmaker Publications, 1976), p. 69.

18. Mather, *The Great Works of Christ in America*, Vol. 2, p. 499.

Chapter 12: Conscience

1. Cited in Joel R. Beeke and Mark Jones, *A Puritan Theology* (Reformation Heritage Books, 2012) p. 911.

2. *Complete Writings*, Vol. 4, pp. 508–09.

3. Cited in Gaustad, *Liberty of Conscience*, p. 213.

4. *Complete Writings*, Vol. 3, pp. 42–43.

5. Cited in Edmund Morgan, *Roger Williams, The Church and the State* (W.W. Norton and Co., 2006), p. 130.

6. James Calvin Davis, *The Moral Theology of Roger Williams* (Westminster John Knox Press, 2004), p. 79.

7. *Complete Writings*, Vol. 1, pp. 98–9.

8. Cited in Davis, *The Moral Theology of Roger Williams*, p. 89.

9. Owen Chadwick, *The Reformation* (Penguin, 1964), p. 403.

10. *Complete Writings*, Vol. 1, p. 136; Vol. 7, p. 243.

11. *Complete Writings*, Vol. 4, pp. 313–14; Vol. 4, pp. 203–04.

12. Knowles, *Memoir of Roger Williams*, p. 370.

13. Larry Siedentop, *Inventing the Individual: The Origins of Western Liberalism* (Penguin, 2015).

14. Raymond Plant, 'Religion in a Liberal State', in *Religion in a Liberal State*, ed. by Gavin D'Costa, Malcolm Evans, Tariq Modood and Julian Rivers (Cambridge University Press, 2013), p. 9.

15. Jocelyn Maclure and Charles Taylor, *Secularism and Freedom of Conscience* (Harvard University Press, 2010).

16. *Complete Writings*, Vol. 4, p. 518.

17. *First Freedom First—Restoring a Civil Public Square for the good of all*: Addresses at SOLAS CPC, St Peter's Free Church of Scotland, Dundee, November 2011.

Chapter 13: Church and State

1. *Correspondence*, Vol. 2, p. 774.

2. *Complete Writings*, Vol. 3, p. 3.

3. Barry, *Roger Williams and the Creation of the American Soul*, p. 346.
4. *Complete Writings*, Vol. 3, p. 184.
5. *Complete Writings*, Vol. 3, p. 158; Vol. 3, pp. 392–97.
6. *Complete Writings*, Vol. 1, p. 392.
7. Timothy Hall, *Separating Church and State* (University of Illinois Press, 1998), pp. 124–32.
8. Os Guinness, *The Case for Civility* (HarperOne, 2008), pp. 73–4.
9. *Complete Writings*, Vol. 3, p. 73; *Correspondence*, Vol. 2, p. 423.
10. Symington, *Messiah the Prince*, pp. 264–65.
11. Guinness, *The Case for Civility*, pp. 88, 116, 135.
12. Guinness, *The Case for Civility*, p. 10.

Chapter 14: Civility, Natural Law and Pluralism

1. *Complete Writings*, Vol. 3, p. 247.
2. *Complete Writings*, Vol. 4, p. 365.
3. *Complete Writings*, Vol. 4, p. 208.
4. *Complete Writings*, Vol. 7, p. 263.
5. *Complete Writings*, Vol. 3, p. 63.
6. *Complete Writings*, Vol. 3, p. 160.
7. Davis, *The Moral Theology of Roger Williams*, p 111.
8. *Complete Writings*, Vol. 4, pp. 485–87.
9. Davis, *The Moral Theology of Roger Williams*, p. 96.
10. *Complete Writings*, Vol. 7, pp. 203–04.
11. *Complete Writings*, Vol. 3, p. 178.
12. Atheists could not be trusted because they did not believe in God and therefore could not take an oath; Roman Catholics, because they owed prior allegiance to Rome.
13. Bejan, *Mere Civility*, pp. 14, 165.
14. Bejan, *Mere Civility*, p. 153.
15. Bejan, *Mere Civility*, pp. 158, 166.
16. Bejan, *Mere Civility*, pp. 173, 174.
17. *Complete Writings*, Vol. 3, p. 13.
18. Miroslav Volf, *Flourishing: Why we need Religion in a Globalized World* (Yale University Press, 2015), p. 154.

19. Guinness, *The Case for Civility*, pp. 10, 113.

20. Guinness, *The Case for Civility*, pp. 136–37.

21. For the 'two kingdom' position see David VanDrunen, *Natural law and the Two Kingdoms* (Eerdmans 2010) and David VanDrunen, *Living in Two Kingdoms* (Crossway, 2010). For a 'one kingdom' critique see Ryan McIlhenny, *Kingdoms Apart*, (P&R Publishing, 2012). See also a useful discussion in Dan Strange, 'Not ashamed! The Sufficiency of Scripture for Public Theology', *Foundations* 61.1 (2011).

Chapter 15: What Williams Means For Us Today

1. Lyndal Roper, *Martin Luther: Renegade and Prophet* (Vintage, 2016), p. 422.

2. Carolina was formally divided into North and South in 1712.

3. Barry, *Roger Williams and the Creation of the American Soul*, p. 392.

4. W.K. Jordan, *The Development of Religious Toleration in England* (Harvard University Press, 1932), p. 475. Direct influence on the philosopher is difficult to prove. We do not know if he read Williams; Williams' view of liberty was, as we have seen, wider than Locke's. However by the late 1650s Williams' arguments, along with those of the Levellers and Milton, had become widely disseminated even though still far from mainstream. In some form Locke will have come across them. Professor John Coffey in personal correspondence suggests that 'Locke's achievement, from one angle, is to make radical Protestant ideas about religious liberty intellectually respectable.'

5. Gaustad, *Liberty of Conscience*, p. 193.

6. Mather, *The Great Works of Christ*, Vol. 2, p. 495; Gaustad, *Liberty of Conscience*, p. 200.

7. Martha Nussbaum, *Liberty of Conscience: In Defense of America's Tradition of Religious Equality* (Basic Books, 2008).

8. Hall, *Separating Church and State*, p. 166.

9. Barry, *Roger Williams and the Creation of the American Soul*, p. 346.

10. *Complete Writings*, Vol. 4, p. 518.

Appendix: Roger Williams and the Conversion of Native Americans

1. *Correspondence*, Vol. 1, p. 8.

2. *Correspondence*, Vol. 1, p. 102.

3. *Correspondence*, Vol. 1, p. 146.

4. *Complete Writings*, Vol. 1, p. 155.
5. Mather, *The Great Works of Christ in America*, Vol. 2, p. 553.
6. Mather, *The Great Works of Christ in America*, Vol. 2, p. 555.
7. *Complete Writings*, Vol. 1, p. 25.
8. *Complete Writings*, Vol. 1, pp. 86–87.
9. *Complete Writings*, Vol. 1, pp. 86–88.
10. *Complete Writings*, Vol. 1, p. 81, note 15.
11. *Complete Writings*, Vol. 7, p. 37.
12. *Complete Writings*, Vol. 4, p. 369.
13. *Complete Writings*, Vol. 1, pp. 220–21.
14. *Complete Writings*, Vol. 4, pp. 370–71.
15. *Complete Writings*, Vol. 4, pp. 373–74.
16. *Complete Writings*, Vol. 5, p. 447. I have added enumeration and words in square brackets.
17. *Correspondence*, Vol. 1, p. 144.
18. *Correspondence*, Vol. 2, pp. 409, 411.
19. Fisher, Lemons and Mason-Brown, *Decoding Roger Williams*, pp. 78–9.
20. *Correspondence*, Vol. 2, p. 413.
21. *Correspondence*, Vol. 2, pp. 413, 577.
22. *Complete Writings*, Vol. 2, p. 43.
23. *Correspondence*, Vol. 2, p. 410.
24. Fisher, Lemons and Mason-Brown, *Decoding Roger Williams*, p. 42.